Born Again
DAUGHTERS OF ZION

Born Again DAUGHTERS OF ZION

Our Transformational Stories of Revelation, Resilience, and Recovery

LaVerne M. Perlie

BORN AGAIN DAUGHTERS OF ZION
Published by Purposely Created Publishing Group™

Copyright © 2018 LaVerne M. Perlie

All rights reserved.

No part of this book may be reproduced, distributed or transmitted in any form by any means, graphic, electronic, or mechanical, including photocopy, recording, taping, or by any information storage or retrieval system, without permission in writing from the publisher, except in the case of reprints in the context of reviews, quotes, or references.

Printed in the United States of America
ISBN: 978-1-949134-57-5

Special discounts are available on bulk quantity purchases by book clubs, associations and special interest groups. For details email: sales@publishyourgift.com or call (888) 949-6228.
For information log on to www.PublishYourGift.com

Dedication

This book is dedicated to Reverend Vanessa "Van" Coffey who truly devoted her life to empowering, transforming, educating, and mentoring young women in difficult places. God gave her a burning desire to establish a ministry for young women assisting them in a holistic approach to ministry and life. Reverend Coffey was a retired Human Resources Director skilled in Organizational Development Management. She earned her wings before we could work together on this. Rest in Heaven my reverend, sister, doctor, lady, friend.

May 29, 1959–May 11, 2016

Table of Contents

Foreword by Tieshena Davis..................ix

Preface..................xi

Chapter 1: What the Enemy Meant for Evil:
Don't Give Up Too Soon!
Linda Caldwell-Boykin..................17

Chapter 2: Living Mosaic: The Beauty in Brokenness
Carla FB McCray..................15

Chapter 3: I Thought I Could Never Live Again
Pastor Jackqueline R. Easley..................29

Chapter 4: Transforming from Ladybug to
God's Lady
Lady Tawanda Holmes..................41

Chapter 5: Life on Earth Is Preparation for Glory
Michelle Baylor..................55

Chapter 6: "IT"
Arvinese I. Reid..................69

Chapter 7: Making Lemonade
Paula M. Grange..................81

Chapter 8: Damaged Goods
LaVerne M. Perlie..................95

Conclusion..................109

Sources..................111

About the Authors..................113

Foreword

REVELATION.

It is easy to suffer in silence. The general feeling when we are suffering is that no one will understand or no one will care. And although God hears our suffering, for many of us He becomes a source for blame, instead of a source of refuge. We believe that since he knows our hearts, our trials, and our tragedies that he should immediately come to our rescue and automatically fix our circumstances.

The glory of God is in *our faith* in His work, believing and trusting that He will fix it for us in his time. *Born Again Daughters of Zion* is filled with real testimonies from women who have witnessed that faith in God is indeed the beginning of healing and restoration from the most dire and shocking situations.

RESILIENCE.

I was asked to write this foreword because of the tragic circumstances I faced early in my life. Before the age of 11, I was abandoned, abused, deceived, and mistreated by those who should've protected me. Then between the ages of 11–16, I continuously encountered one bad situation after another, and much of it was beyond my control. I prayed to God to fix my situation. And when my prayers were not immediately answered, I shunned him, and instead of praying for deliverance, I prayed for death. But the great thing about God is that he doesn't always give us what we *want*; but he always gives us what we *need*. He gave me life!

RECOVERY.

But more importantly, the moment He provided a way out for me, I made up my mind to *be better* than what my circumstances dictated. My adversity became the cornerstone of my redemption and triumph. I learned that God allows adversity, not to break us, but to strengthen and inspire us! It forces us to go beyond existing and to instead live full lives that glorify him, using the gifts we were given. It also teaches us to rely not on ourselves and our limited knowledge, but to rely on God and His infinite wisdom.

Be encouraged as you read the stories in the pages that follow. Let the narratives minister to your heart and give you a newfound perspective on just what God can do.

Remember that *faith in your deliverance* is the key to your recovery!

Tieshena Davis
Bestselling Author of *Surviving Shocking Situations: Finding Courage to Succeed in Spite Life's of Painful Moments*
www.AskTieDavis.com

PREFACE

Were you once neglected, disjointed, and rejected? Did you feel inadequate, wounded, and cast aside because of your past? I can relate to all of these feelings. I smiled, affirmed, and encouraged others, hoping that no one would see the real me, the me that few people knew (or so I thought). On December 23, 1990, I experienced an awakening while in a public restroom. I decided that I no longer wanted to be in the state that I was in. I remember praying and asking God to help me. And He did just that. He ushered me into a transformational journey of restoration and wholeness. Once I called out to him: I sought the Lord and He heard me and delivered me from all of my fears (Psalm 34:4 KJV).

> He wiped away all of my tears, spoke life into my ears,
>
> Gave me strength and power, He covers me by the hour
>
> Released me from my pain, and the grip of those chains
>
> I shared my victory, celebrated my release, now I have peace

> I took authority over my life, I closed the door of my past,
>
> I changed my mindset and actions, opened the door to my future,
>
> and strutted right into my destiny.

Have you closed the door? If not, this book will help you close the door(s) on poor self-esteem, shame, brokenness, and all other things that have you bound. What I know for sure is that, you were not meant to self-destruct, nor be an outcast! Everyone must travel a path in life. Some pathways are rocky, rough, and filled with obstacles. All are necessary to help you reach your destination. No matter who you are, what you were, or what you've done, the road to peace awaits you. Every new beginning is compatible to a birth. My birthing process began with a promise, followed by healing, recovery, restoration, and wholeness. I told another sister, and she told another, and she told another, and now we're telling others.

Born Again Daughters of Zion (BADZ) are women who have encountered a rebirth experience after overcoming adversities in life. BADZ have accepted their rightful place as daughters of God. BADZ are those women who decided to take authority over their past hurts, setbacks, and offenses, which at one time halted their progression in life. BADZ boldly declare and decree total annihilation to the enemy's plans of sabotage over their lives. BADZ are recipients of God's omni-beneficent grace, have embraced HIS peace, and were chosen for a time such as this to tell their compelling stories of empowerment and recovery to the nations! Within this book you'll learn about the transformational stories written by eight dynamic women who are now living life to the fullest and are advancing in their purpose.

Jeremiah 30:17 (NIV)

But I will restore you to health and heal your wounds, declares the Lord, because you are called an outcast, Zion for whom no one cares.

I AM UNASHAMED

I AM RESTORED

I AM DELIVERED

I AM HEALED

I AM A BORN AGAIN DAUGHTER OF ZION

Chapter 1

What the Enemy Meant for Evil Don't Give Up Too Soon!

Linda Caldwell-Boykin

In my childhood I remember being very quiet and timid. I was often unable to voice my feelings or share my thoughts with others, which caused me to suppress my emotions. I was raised in a two-parent household with a solid upbringing where everything I needed was provided for me. I knew I was loved. However, we never expressed it verbally with "I love you." We rarely communicated or acknowledged negative incidents or episodes that occurred within the family. It was made clear, "What goes on in this house stays in this house." This learned behavior would eventually become a detriment to my life. I learned to suppress my feelings and stifle my voice to the magnitude where everything stayed bottled up inside. To add injury to insult, I recall dealing with an insurmountable level of rejection among my peers. Often, we would play games such as kickball and baseball with the neighborhood kids where teams were selected. I wanted to fit in, but I was constantly the last one chosen to play. These kinds of incidents occurred on a regular basis. Because of this rejection I developed an intense need to be accepted, coupled with identity crisis. Many negative outside forces and voices began to shape my mental and emotional capacity to believe in myself. These kinds of encounters early on, set the stage for some spiraling events to occur throughout my teenage and young adult years. These unstable foundations had a tremendous impact on my self-perception and self-esteem, which ultimately led to self-sabotage. No matter what kind of success or victories I obtained there was always that inner voice (self-talk) that told me I wasn't good enough, nobody likes you, you're not pretty enough, you can't do this or that, and nobody will ever love you. I became accustomed to wearing a mask to anesthetize the pain. I looked good on the outside but was tormented on the inside, secretly comparing myself to others. At some point, I concluded that my inner voices where right and I agreed. Maybe you can identify with some of the same issues. If so, I want to inform you the final verdict on your life isn't in yet. Don't close the curtain. Your show is not over. Your vision may be a little impaired by what you're going through, but there is a way out.

Once the pain became great enough, I started seeking other ways to numb what I felt inside. I was introduced to marijuana by a group of my peers and the day I tried it, to my recollection, everything subsided for what seemed like forever. In reality, the pain was diminished only for a short period of time. But as evil would have it, the euphoric feeling soothed me and I believed that I was all right. I felt as if I finally fit in with my peers. There were no demands to be met, no judgments; we were parallel, at least in the beginning. New relationships began to form with the opposite sex and emotional dynamics came into play. Because I was already emotionally unhealthy, I cultivated unstable affiliations that were detrimental. Consumed by the necessity to be accepted, loved, and needed I found myself entangled in numerous relationships that left me feeling abandoned and alone. These partnerships were the inception of a viscous revolving cycle of addiction, heartbreak, and denial.

I began to experiment with other illicit drugs. My acquaintances changed and I was introduced to PCP. It seemed to numb the hurt I felt on the inside. I remember the euphoric out-of-body experience I had the very first time. I thought I could conquer just about anything; but once again, deception had me in its grip. For a long period of time, I was able to function while using, keeping a job and going to school. I partied all night, showered, changed clothes, and made it to my destination on time. But slowly, things began to catch up with me and my discipline waned. My addiction took a front row seat in my life. Overtaken by the obsession to use and the need to feel good, I began to experiment even more. You name it I tried it! Then, around the age of nineteen, I was introduced to crack cocaine and began to spiral out of control. The Devil had a plot, but God had a plan. I was totally out of my league. Evil had infiltrated my life with one of its highest and best ranking generals with heavy artillery. Satan came to kill, steal and destroy (John 10:10 KJV). Things happened so fast once the spiral began. I lost my job and left school. My mind was consumed with the thought of my next high. Completely numb, I sought out strategies and opportunities to supply my habit. I had to have it by any means necessary. I had a habit that needed to be supported and I was not going to be without. Consequently, I made acquaintances with dealers and those who operated in street pharmaceuticals (illicit drugs). I made drops and sales for street dealers. It became the source of supplying my daily habit without having to depend on others. Unfortunately, what started as a resource became an addiction as well. I was equally as consumed with merchandising as I was using. I told myself countless times "today is the last day," but evil had a hold on me. The hole seemed to get deeper and deeper, darker and darker, and it was swallowing me up fast.

    Once I began selling, I had several episodes with the law. I never will forget the first time I was incarcerated as result of serving drugs to an undercover policeman.

The experience was a real nightmare. The only thing I knew about jail was what I had heard. But I found myself handcuffed in the back of a police car being transported to the police department holding cell. I was searched, finger printed, given a cold bologna sandwich with juice, and placed in a holding cell for the night. After seeing the commissioner in court, I was released on my own recognizance with a court date to return. This tormenting cycle continued for several years and threatened the very core of my life. I fell deeper into despair and was bound by demonic strongholds, broken hearted, wounded in soul and spirit with no hope of a way out. I was convinced that I would probably die in that state, and I governed myself according to what I that belief. Self-destruction became my best friend and self-deception was its twin. I longed to return to some place of normalcy, but I was traveling through life lost. My days were spent in crack houses where the living conditions were unfit for anyone. I stayed up for days at a time without sleeping or eating. I even overdosed a few times. One time in particular, I had been indulging for days and I passed out. I remember seeing my whole life flash before my eyes up to that very moment. Fear gripped me, and I woke up physically fighting, soaking wet. Someone had picked me up, placed me in the tub, and ran cold water from the shower over me. It brought me back. Thank God! Many days I prayed, "Lord please help me and take these evil desires away from me." It seemed for such a long time that God was not listening. I was in a place where no human flesh could rescue, help, or deliver me. In my heart I knew that if I ever got out, it would only be by the power of God. I was twenty-five years old and had practiced this lifestyle for 13 years. I increased my drug intake trying to ease the thoughts in my mind about the possibilities of being caught by the police. My track record with the law had become quite extensive. I had several open cases in the court system and for one of them, I didn't show up. A warrant was issued for my arrest.

On December 12, 1989, I remember feeling overwhelmingly tired, weary, and so broken from the weight of running, hiding, cheating, lying and all that comes with that lifestyle. Satan spoke loudly to my mind saying, "You're going to die like this." I was done, overtaken with evil thoughts in my mind, and once again I agreed with my adversary. As always, when those demonic forces would attack me I would behave accordingly and follow-up with choices that coincided with my state of mind. BUT GOD!

I had yet another run in with the law. But this one would become the conduit God would use to change my entire life forever. I sold drugs to another undercover police officer and within seconds police cars appeared from everywhere. Taken by surprise, I stood there bewildered and relieved all at the same time. I was arrested by the angels in blue and I remember like it was yesterday that as they handcuffed me, a sigh of relief came over me. I faintly whispered the words, "I'm so tired." It was at that moment that I knew God had not only heard my prayers, but He answered them too. I would love to tell you that everything immediately got better, but I cannot. However, it was the beginning of an end. After being processed into the correctional facility, the first thirty days were chaotic. My mind was totally consumed with thoughts of using and getting out of there. Desperation set in and I made connections with those who had similar thoughts. As a matter of fact, it was easy to fall directly into the same old street behavior patterns right in the facility. The Devil had a plot, but God had a plan.

After lying in that cell for about a month, I had a breakthrough. Finally, I came to a pivotal point in my life, with one thought in my mind that would lead me to victories I could never have imagined. I said to myself, "You are better than this." Being told what to do, confined and limited in my freedom, and missing my family made me I realize that I deserved better for myself. From this, I'm reminded of the parable of the Prodigal Son in the Bible; I came to myself. From that time forth, my eyes opened and my perception changed. Although it may have been motivated by the fact that I wanted to be released to go home, it was enough to cause me to rise from the ashes.

I made my mind up that I was going to stop using and start preparing myself for my court date. I did this despite being presented the opportunity to use recreational drugs even while incarcerated. I started going to school to get my GED, knowing that it would show I was making an effort to change. School occupied my time and distracted my mind from focusing too much on home. In the end, I was hoping the judge would have mercy on me and allow me to receive probation because I was a first-time offender without any prior convictions. But I must admit that in the beginning, my motives were not entirely pure. I just wanted to get out of my situation and not be sentenced to jail time. God truly knows the heart of man. There were so many different people talking to me about my outcome and what the results would be that I believed that my chances of going home looked pretty good.

My court date finally arrived, and one of the things that sticks out in my mind is that all the people I ran with, sold drugs for, and called my friends were not in the court room that day. There was only my mom sitting there on my behalf, the one who always took my collect calls and sent funds when she had extra money. She was there to see me through. The judge called my case and I stood as he looked over the facts. He then asked if I had anything to say. I gave him my best foot forward speech and when it was sentencing time, I crossed my fingers behind my back, anxiously awaiting the verdict. The judge proceeded to speak about the progress I had made in such short time. I thought, "Okay, here it comes. He's going to release me to probation." But that was not so. He gave me a twenty-month to five-year sentence and said that since I was doing so well, he wanted me to continue my progress. My heart fell to the ground. I had never been to prison before or away from my family. Although my family was deeply hurt by my addiction they still loved me and always supported me. I was numb with shock. I didn't know if I was angry, hurt, scared or confused; all I knew was that I wouldn't be going home that day or any day in my near future. But I knew it was God once again looking out for me. I had to be locked-up to be set free.

I was transported back to the county jail, and drenched in devastation, decided to just lay down. I cried myself to sleep and fell off into a dream where I saw myself floating through the air dressed in all white. It jolted me awake and I sat straight up in the bed. As I opened my eyes I heard my name called and the gate of my cell was opening. The guard had come to inform me I was being transferred to Lorton Correctional Facility. No more county jail. I was headed into the federal prison system. God was changing my direction. I was headed into unchartered territory and my only hope was to trust that God was with me. Once I arrived at my new destination, I found that most of the people I knew from the neighborhood were there too. In one regard, it was comforting to have people I knew already there. On the other hand, I didn't want any bad influences around me. I had decided that I would give myself a chance, one hundred percent, since I had to be there. I would give my all to change myself and my situation.

After being there for a while I was able to see my family face to face, which helped me a great deal. It strengthened me to know that they could come and see me at least once a month. I had hope that I could make it through. I continued to make progress and there in the prison, God began to restore one of my gifts. The women liked looking halfway decent even though they were in prison. This gave me the opportunity to use my cosmetology skills. I would do the ladies' hair in exchange sweets, food, and cigarettes from commissary. I did not exchange my services for drugs, although the option was available to me. The desire to use had dissipated and I wanted it to stay that way. I started to believe that things may not be as bad as I thought. As long as I could see family and have some kind of normalcy; I could make it.

One day a young lady came to me and said, "Linda you're being transferred out of here tonight." I thought, surely not me. I don't have a long enough sentence to be transported to another federal correctional facility. I asked her how she knew and she told me that she had been cleaning the captain's office and saw my name on the transfer list for that night. Everyone waited up that night to see who was going. I styled hair until close to midnight when I finally just decided to go to bed. But the moment I lay down, they called my name for transfer. I was off to Alderson, West Virginia where I did the remainder of my time. In spite of the unknown, God walked with me through every step of the reconstruction process.

In Alderson, the rules changed. They offered a lot more to inmates through programs and work details to help with rehabbing their lives. I took total advantage of these avenues and enrolled in school to complete my GED and several life skill classes as well. My relationship with Christ seemed to be growing stronger and stronger. Prison is where God revealed Himself to me. I sought to get a factory job where they would pay three hundred dollars a month, but God had other plans. Instead of the factory job, I received a job cleaning the chapel on campus for five dollars a month. God was beginning to mold me for greater task ahead. I took pride in cleaning the chapel so that others would have a nice place to come and meet with the Lord. After all, He met me there constantly. The chapel priest gave me another opportunity, asking if I was interested in joining the choir. I could not resist. I had grown up singing because my dad sang in a quartet for over forty years. They gave me a robe; I was officially on the choir. For the first time in my life I belonged to something that had real purpose. I had found a place where I fit—in the house of God.

I gave my life to Christ and my spiritual life took off. My prayer life increased and I studied the word of God regularly. My thinking began to transform with hope for a brighter future. God met me right where I was in the darkest time of my life. I served God faithfully during my time of incarceration, and after serving eighteen months, was released to a halfway house in the District of Columbia where I was acclimated back into society. I complied with all the rules of the halfway house and after about nine months, I was released on what they called home monitoring program. I had made my mind up that I was going to stay with God during this process. I would live a very structured life style for quite some time as I slowly made the transition. I worked, began to mend family ties, and found a church to join and served. My faith had grown stronger and I didn't even think about the monitoring device that was placed on my leg. I was just glad to go home. I continued to grow in Christ and shortly thereafter, I was taken off the monitoring system to finish my time on parole for 5 years. I was home, back in the neighborhood where I had actively practiced using, this time to be a light in darkness for others who had a desire to change. I would be a testament to those who were still suffering a life of addiction. I had through every part of the correctional system, but God was securing my future and assuring that I would never return to that system or the lifestyle again.

It's been over twenty-five years since that time, and God has elevated me in so many ways that I can't fit it all in one chapter. But what I will say is that through it all, God made a way for me. You may feel like you are buried underneath some obstacles that are not favorable right now. Maybe it's plagued you for many years. But I can tell you to expect a miracle in your situation. God could be positioning you. Anything is possible when conditions are just right for God. Before my stay in prison, I had no idea that God was setting things up to bless me with a future that I was incapable of seeing at the time. So be encouraged in the eye of the storm. If you are feeling like your life is shattered, broken, with no hope of a way out, I am a witness that what the enemy meant for evil; God will work out for your good. You may be down today, but don't you give up. God has a plan designed just for you.

Chapter 2

Living Mosaic: The Beauty in Brokenness

Carla FB McCray

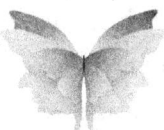

To all who mourn in Israel, he will give a crown of beauty for ashes, a joyous blessing instead of mourning, festive praise instead of despair. In their righteousness, they will be like great oaks that the LORD has planted for his own glory.

—Isaiah 61:3

Each day of our lives becomes a new piece of colored glass or stone added to our living mosaic. The individual stones and glass differ in shape, color, and texture, with some offering high and low transparency or smooth and sharp edges that denote the high and low points of our lives. There are times that we are blessed to add the pieces to our artwork ourselves; however, in other times, pieces are added by others and life situations that we are unable to control. Either way, whether in high or low points in our lives, we can look at our mosaic and say it's beautiful. But what happens when you have spent years creating this work of art and it is dropped suddenly, shattering into many pieces. You look down to see that some pieces of stones and glass are still in tack and whole and others crumbled and unrecognizable. How do you begin to pick up the pieces? How do you begin to put your life back together again?

Many of us go through our lives prearranging our calendars in advance with the expectation and hope that what's planned will happen. We get up with our normal routines set in place. But someday, unforeseen things may arise. I can speak for most people when I say that we don't go through our day-to-day expecting tragedy. For instance, there are times when we may be aware that a loved one has fallen ill, and although it's tough at the time of death, we were given some time to spend with them before they cross over. But tragedy is different. It's unforeseen. And when it occurs, it immediately takes your breath away. I will never forget the day when tragedy struck my life and left me feeling like my life had ended then started over as if it had never existed.

As the hospital elevator moved I stared at the numbers highlighting one by one, waiting for it to stop at my designated floor. It was weird, almost unexplainable, but it was as if a piece of me left while I was in the elevator. Ding! It stopped at my floor and then the doors opened. I stepped out to family and friends whose faces dropped as I walked toward them. With open arms, my father grabbed me and hugged me tight as he whispered in my ear, "Baby girl, he didn't make it through the surgery; he's gone."

On August 21, 2001, at the age of twenty-one, I became a widow, a single mother of one, five months away from delivering baby number two. In addition to being a wife and mother, I was a full-time student and employee when my life suddenly stopped with the unforeseen death of my twenty-one-year-old husband. One day he was here and the next day he was gone. A man of God who was giving, loved life and his family, and who was filled with so much joy was snatched away abruptly by an ultra-rare blood disease called Thrombotic Thrombocytopenic Purpura. This catastrophic event took over my mind, heart, and spirit, and I became stuck in an unfamiliar place. Each day became harder than the next just to move forward. The agony, anger, brokenness, and anxiety began to attach itself to me like weights, until one morning I woke up and was unable to move. As I lie there with tears rolling down the side of my face, I mustered up enough strength to open my mouth to pray, "Lord help me, please! Lift this heaviness, hurt, bitterness, anger, and anxiety off me. Help me to get out of this place. Give me the tools to let go, move forward, and survive because my children need me. Please help me!" There was a calming that instantly came over me, and although I knew I couldn't rewrite the past, it was at that very moment I knew we would be okay.

Acknowledgment and Acceptance

Call me crazy for saying this, but the beautiful thing about my story is that God *didn't* wave a wand over my life like the fairy godmother and instantly change everything. However, God did allow me to go through the process of healing after a tragedy so that I could understand that He can give you beauty for your ashes. In my grief process, I found that tragedy has the power to break you into little pieces, but God can rebuild you and give you a greater strength and resilience. It took me lying in my bed, crippled by pain, depression, and anxiety to realize that it wasn't normal and that I needed help. God led me to acknowledge and accept that tragedy had taken place in my life and that it was present. It had knocked on my door, walked into my life and decided that it wanted to live in my home. When I say home, I am referring to my mind, my spirit, and my body. Acknowledging that an event, whether big or small, has taken place in your life can be difficult. For a long time, I woke up thinking that it was all a dream. And although I knew he wasn't coming back, I found myself mirroring a child, folding my arms with an "I don't want to" attitude. I didn't want to believe that God had taken my husband so soon. I didn't want to believe that he wasn't ever coming back. I didn't want to believe that he would miss all the small and major moments in our children's lives that we discussed and looked forward to. I didn't want to!

As human beings, we develop routines. For instance, we become accustomed to the way we drive to work, how long it takes us to arrive, and even how many parking spots we can expect to be available based on the time we get there. So what happens when we run into a roadblock or a detour? We become irritated that we now must go a different way, that it may take a little longer to arrive, or that we will be late and the parking spot that we typically get will no longer available. The simple things become daunting because it makes us uncomfortable and we find it hard to adjust without emotions. I had to acknowledge not only that tragedy had taken place, but also how this affected me emotionally. No one ever came to me and said, "Carla, you don't look so good," or that I seemed depressed. I often wondered how I could be around people and they not even know or see how I was feeling inside? Although it is extremely important to surround yourself with positive and supportive people during the grieving stage following tragedy, I had to realize that it wasn't the job of my family and friends to recognize how I was truly feeling. I *chose* not to communicate my true feelings. Looking back now and thinking about how many times I was asked, "How are you doing," and I responded, "I am okay," I realize that there were too many days when I should have simply said: "I am not doing so well."

Does this resonate with you? How many times have you chosen not to acknowledge situations in your life and how it has affected you? Why do we do that? Is it because we want people to see an image of us that is "whole and strong" and not "weary and broken"? Is it because we don't want to show a sign of weakness or that we want people to think that we have it all together? I remember saying to myself, "Carla you are strong and you can do this. Pull it together. You are okay." Little did I know that covering my emotions with a bandage was slowly breaking me down. You can sweep your feelings under the rug time after time, but eventually, the pile will start to show.

You must choose to acknowledge and accept your life as it currently is. Ask and believe that God can start unhooking the emotional weights that attached themselves to you because of your life's situation. Doing this will allow you to feel like moving forward is possible and your future is visible and obtainable. Once I made a conscious decision to acknowledge and accept that, God brought me to the serenity prayer written by Reinhold Niebuhr. This prayer allowed me to focus on acknowledgment and acceptance and became the prayer that started and ended my day. The prayer went, "God, grant me the serenity to accept the things I cannot change, courage to change the things I can, and wisdom to know the difference."

Picking up the Pieces

Being able to acknowledge that tragedy has taken place in your life and how it made you feel is a huge accomplishment. But how do you begin piecing your life back together again? There is a Japanese art called "Kintsukuroi" – the art of repairing broken pottery with gold or silver lacquer and understanding that the piece of art is more beautiful for having been broken and put back together again. In our lives, we will be faced with broken moments that I believe are used to build who we become and move us toward our purpose in our life. When I reflect on my moments of brokenness, I can say that every time, without a doubt, there was pain in the process of overcoming. After the death of my husband the remaining five months of my pregnancy felt extremely long and tiring, and it was tough. It was only after visiting my obstetrician that I learned what affect his death was having on me and our unborn daughter. I remember Dr. Pin entering the room, sitting down in his swivel chair, and scooting over to me. Instead of flipping through his chart like he typically did, he grabbed my hands. "Look at me Carla," he said. His eyes were filled with tears and I begin to sob profusely. He said, "I am so sorry for your loss and I cannot imagine what you are going through, but she needs you to fight." As I sniffed, I asked, "Is she okay?"

"Yes," he said. "She looks fine, but Carla you have loss too much weight since your last visit and we don't need any unforeseen situations to occur." He went on to say, "I believe your little girl can feel what you are going through and she is fighting for you. So, you need you to fight for her."

At that moment, the thought of my baby girl's face which I had seen on the ultrasound, and whose heartbeat I heard, would give me strength to get me to her day of delivery. But the joyous moment of finally seeing her face was still filled with pain. Although my family was there for support, it still wasn't the same. My husband wasn't there to hold my hand and tell me to push. He wasn't there to crack jokes to get the through the physical pain I felt, to give me ice chips, or to simply kiss me to tell me what a good job I was doing. The tears I shed that day were mixed with joy and pain, but those tears led me to my final push, delivering a beautiful, healthy baby girl.

Although I could see the grief slowly lifting and my life coming back together, there were still days that I didn't want to be bothered, even by those who I loved most. Other days, I would take time to reflect on the memories, grab a few broken pieces of my life, and add it back as if I was recreating my life's mosaic work of art. I struggled with why God would allow Kenny's life to end so soon, not allowing him to see his children grow up and accomplish all of the things that we discussed and hope for them. I would be angry when I heard stories of men who didn't desire a relationship with their children and who were living their life to the fullest; yet Kenny, who had his son on his hip any time he had a chance, a man who adored his son and the daughter that he would never meet, was cut short on life. But I will never forget the night that became the last night I would be angry or question God. I drifted off into a heavy sleep, and Kenny was there, just as real as this book you are reading, with a big smile on his face. As we walked toward each other he opened his arms and embraced me. For a moment we didn't even speak, just exhaled and embraced each other. I sank into his arms and begin to cry. "Carla don't cry," he said. I looked up to him and told him that I missed him and that I didn't think I could make it without him. He smiled at me, wiping my tears away and said, "But you can."

"But, I would rather you be here with me and our children," I said. But Carla I couldn't stay," he said. I was sick and if I had stayed, I would have stayed at the doctor having transfusion after transfusion and I didn't want it for me, you, or our children. It would have just been too much. So, before I told God I would go, I made Him make me a promise. I asked him to promise me that He would take care of you, Kaelen, and Kaela. I made him promise that you'll will never lack or go without, and God promised me and told me not to worry. So, don't worry. You can make it." We hugged until he told me he had to go and told me to Give Kaelen and Kaela a kiss for him. Holding his hands, a bright light appeared from the sky and he began to ascend. I tried to hold his hands tight and for as long as I could until all that was left were the tips of my fingers touching his. Then his image disappeared into the bright light. When I awakened, my pillow was drenched in tears. I sat up in bed, feeling like the encounter I had just experienced was so real. I felt at peace knowing that Kenny was okay, and had told me not to worry because we would be okay. From that day forward, I stopped asking the question how and why and instead embraced the beautiful memories that I shared with my husband, which helped me piece my life back together again. After a tragedy, some people never get their life back. They are so stricken with grief that they are unable to overcome, and they become forever stuck in the same place they were when tragedy hit. This is not God's desire for us. His desire is that through every situation we overcome, grow, learn, and are strengthened so that we can help someone else along the way.

You must start looking at the full perspective of your life. I had to let of everything that kept me bound and unable to move forward go. I didn't want anyone to recreate my living mosaic for me because no one knew my life like I did. You know how it goes. Some people will take your situations and recreate them, good or bad, into what they believe your life is or should be. There is only one person who knows me, my life, and how it will end, and that's God. So, knowing that God was with me, I had to understand that this was my opportunity to pick up my own pieces and rebuild my life, the life that at one point I thought that I would never see again.

So, where can you find beauty in the midst of picking up the broken pieces of your life? The beauty lies in the moment you yield and say that although I am afraid and hurting, I can longer allow this situation to steal my joy and my peace. I can no longer allow the broken pieces to lie around as if they never were a part of my life. Beauty is in the moment when you yield to God and say I am letting go so that you can mend my heart, restore my mind, strengthen my spirit, and put me back together. The beauty is in the moment that you find an inner strength that you never realized existed to fight for your life again although you don't know what the future holds. The beauty is in overcoming. You'll be able to look back at those moments of brokenness, that unexpected detour in your life and say, "God, I didn't like the pain, but what I gained from it was worth it. Thank you, God, for giving me this opportunity to recreate my living mosaic. I am stronger, wiser and better because of it and I am grateful."

Transformation

It has always been amazing to me how God can change a mess into a miracle. Transformation is defined as a thorough or dramatic change in form or appearance. After deciding to pick up the broken pieces of your life and start recreating your living mosaic, transformation starts to take place. It is here in your life that you can begin seeing piece by piece how your life is coming back together. The thing that shattered your life and made a mess becomes a miracle. You have the potential to transform disappointing moments in your life into positive moments. It is here that you can reflect on your experiences. You can help others that may be going through similar situations and feel a sense of accomplishment that your moment of brokenness was for a reason and for a greater good. You understand that your life's situations were tough, but were bigger than you. I met countless young ladies who were single mothers working hard to sustain. Although none of them had lost a husband, they were raising their children on their own and juggling life as it came to them. I felt empowered because I could now look back to my countless moments of weakness or wanting to give up—moments of pressing my way through work and school, still attending every game, parent conference, or PTA meeting. I learned that I could make it and it was important for me to encourage other women to do the same. Being able to encourage them to keep pushing at moments when they wanted to give up gave me the sense that my pain was for a purpose.

The beauty in transforming your broken pieces into your living mosaic is that you will find buried treasures that you never knew where there. I never knew that at the age of 21 my life would stop abruptly and I would literally have to fight off depression. When I was going through it, I didn't see a way out or that I could even make it. But God would allow me to have an encounter that would change my life forever. That encounter helped me see the elements, layers, and hidden strengths within me that I never knew existed. I believe that these treasures were placed within us before the beginning of time. God knows and already understands every moment of our lives. He knows that there will be things that we may need along the way to survive tough moments. The treasures that God buried within me were strength, patience, and independence. He knew that the process of getting married and suddenly becoming a widowed mother of two would require inner strength to endure, survive, and overcome. Although I am now remarried, God knew that it would require a lot of patience to be a single mother, juggling work and my children's schooling and activities. God knew that this journey would require me to develop true independence. Although I had supportive friends and family, there were some moments of this process that I could only go through, confront, and accomplish alone. There are treasures within us that are still lying dormant, developing within for moments that we have yet to experience and that we have not even tapped into. How amazing is that?

Your living mosaic is an ongoing piece of art that will continue to be added to each day. A masterpiece takes time to create and has various elements that are added to reflect its beauty. Whether you like it or not, there are moments when you have to start over or recreate, but in the end it's your masterpiece. God has been with you during the entire process of creating your living mosaic—guiding, strengthening, removing, restoring and transforming your life every step of the way. He doesn't stop there. Although we are not perfect, He is all knowing and forgiving, and chooses when our living mosaic is finalized. The jagged edges, moments that pierced your heart, and the smooth pieces that mended it back together are covered. He mends every piece of stone and glass together to ensure that there are no cracks left unsealed and no edges left untouched. Your masterpiece is whole. You will be able to take a step back and see the beauty that has developed from the ends and outs and ups and downs in your life. And although beautiful, you will find yourself amazed that God took the areas of your life that looked like they didn't belong and somehow managed to make fit. An imperfect living mosaic is made perfect in the eyes of God.

Trials and tribulations will come, but remember that God always makes everything good in His timing. When there are moments that you feel like you cannot go on, remember that God has buried treasures within that are tailor-made for you. It is His desire to see that you live a healed, whole, and free life. Take this moment to reflect on your life, your trials and triumphs, what was produced through Gods healing, and who you have become because of it. God doesn't make mistakes, rather He produces miracles. Always remember anything can be broken, but the beauty is in the art that is produced in the end.

Chapter 3

I Thought I Could Never Live Again

Pastor Jackqueline R. Easley

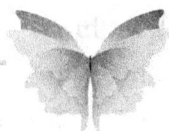

I have always known that the Lord is watching out for me, but there was one day, one tragic day, when I doubted if He cared about me. After experiencing the hardest struggle in my life, I doubted God. But today I know that my God is nigh to me when I seek him and he is listening to my earnest cry. Jeremiah 29:12 (KJV) declares, when I call on the Lord in prayer, he will hearken unto me and when I seek the Lord, I will find him.

On a rainy day in April 2006, away in Las Vegas, I got a phone call that changed my whole life. Prior to this phone call I had had a dream that my son was in trouble and God took me to a beautiful place as I spoke to my son. I had no idea that the phone call that would wake me would be the emergency department where I work, saying my son had been shot in the head and I needed to get home right away. It was 3 a.m. Las Vegas time when I was awakened by this phone call and I wondered whether I was still dreaming or if it was real. Tears began to run down my face and I was speechless. I heard the voice on the phone saying, "Get home right away, hopefully your son will be here when you get here. We need you to consent for surgery! Who can we call?" As I scrolled through my phone to call my family in Baltimore, I screamed loudly in the darkness of my hotel room, "Lord don't take my son. I can't live without him."

The Lord was looking out for me even in that moment. My Aunt Patricia was in Las Vegas with me and as I picked up the phone to call her, the phone rang and she told me to get to the airport immediately. She had already booked my flight. I went home from Las Vegas with anger, sadness, pain, and every emotion imaginable, wondering what I did wrong, what my last conversation with my son was, and asking God to let him live for me to see him and talk to him. I became angry with God and overwhelmed by guilt because I was not there to save my son. On the ride home, all I could do was think about his childhood and what I could have done differently. If I had stayed with his father would things be different? How would I be able to live with myself if my son, Shelton, did not make it?

I made it to the hospital and into the Neurology Critical Care Unit, where I would see my son. When I arrived on the floor, the waiting room was packed with friends and family showing support for me. But at the time, all I could see was the pathway to my son's room. I walked in and the moment I saw him I felt myself descending into a wilderness of anger, pain, guilt, and sorrow. All I could think about is that this was my baby. He was only 20 years old and he had no children. He loved everyone. "Why my child?" I asked. "What did I do?" I screamed at God, "Lord you telling me you are taking my child?" I wanted to die. I asked God to take my life and let my son live. If I could have traded places with him, I would have. This stay in the neurology critical care unit opened many wounds, because not only was my son fighting for his life, but his father and his wife were there, and this was a wound that was still open and fresh.

The longest two days of my life were in the halls and room of that critical care unit. There was family everywhere and people praying, but all I could do was go deeper into my wilderness of emotions. Have you ever had many people around, but your problems made you feel like you were all alone? This is how I felt in those moments. Have you ever been in a wilderness and when you look back, you can remember the day you slipped into that horrible place? I was there for many years.

My son lost his battle to violence two days later, and as I picked up the pieces of my heart and left the hospital to go home and plan his funeral, a shocking detail was revealed. I found out that my son had been shot at my paternal aunt's house. This not only caused hate in my heart, but tension between my families. I found myself with hate toward someone who had absolutely nothing to do with my son being shot. I lived with this hatred for many years after the incident and I felt my anger living through my other children. I saw my children, my youngest brother, and my godson year after year on my son's anniversary, displaying this anger, frustration, sorrow, and disappointment. We would celebrate with alcohol every year and cry, reliving the day my son transitioned. The way we celebrated forced each one of us to relive the painful experience and to go deeper and deeper into the wilderness that I would one day need to be delivered from. Why didn't I know this? Because the enemy wanted to keep me bound and handcuffed to my emotions. Think about your situation and how many times you've allowed the enemy to keep you trapped in a wilderness and reliving painful experiences that keep you in bondage.

I left God and I left the church because I was mad with God. "Why did you take my son?" I asked. "I will not serve you. Why couldn't you spare my child? And now you want me to preach and do your will?" This is how I truly felt at the time, and yes I talked to God that way and wanted him to give me an answer to my questions. For years I lived in a world of my own, doing everything I could do to curse God and not do his will. The one thing I can say to you is that even though I left God, he never left me alone to fight my demons. There were times when I tried to kill myself because of the guilt that I held because of my son's death. I believed it was because I was not a good mother and that maybe I should have done things differently. This continued for at least seven years, 24 hours a day, wanting to die and not being able to think clearly and know my life was worth living. I really thought I could never live again. I thought I could never face the world again. I thought I could never be happy. Today, I thank God for his grace and mercy that always pushed me and covered me even when I turned my back on Him.

After every tragedy, there is a time when God will bring you out, and the Lord has already placed people who will be instrumental in your deliverance. My mother was my biggest encourager and she knew I was not happy with the way things had evolved. God knew my mother and my uncle would be the ones to get me back to the altar. I fought them all the way back, but God had appointed a time for my deliverance, and that time came. "Not another phone call! I would think to myself. When it was my mother, I'd ask "What does she want this time," while thinking, " I'm not going over to that church with her." These are the thoughts I had every time my mother would call to ask me to go to church with her. But there came a day when the call felt different, because my uncle needed me and I could never tell him no. As I reflect on the call, I know that God was indeed still steering the wheel, guiding me. I finally said yes.

I walked into the church once again, and as I sat in the pew, an unexplainable feeling encapsulated me. I felt my son's presence and I felt God again after being in a wilderness for over seven years. I sat in that church on the third row from the back with the tears flowing down my face thinking, "I cannot do this." I thought, "God you took my son, you took my dad, and you took my stepdad." The year of 2006 was the worst year of my life and the most challenging. In a span of three months, I lost my son, my biological dad, and then my dad who had raised me from the age of three. So all I could think about is the fact that God had taken everyone away from me. I told God, "I will not come back for you to take anyone else from me. I don't want this." But the more I said "No" and "I can't," the more I kept hearing God say, "YES!" I felt the power of the Holy Spirit starting to work on me from the inside out and I started going to church every week. At first, my prayers were very short and unattached, but I know the Lord heard my cry because I could feel that he was starting to reside within me again. For a while, I was in the church but living in that same wilderness because I had not allowed God to heal me completely. You might be asking me how. I am a witness that when you harbor hate and anger in your heart without full disclosure, transparency, and deliverance, you walk around defeated and living in your yesterday. But as my prayer life increased and I intertwined with the Lord, I began to empty out of self and seek God for healing. I began asking God how I could be delivered from my wilderness and what I needed to do. Have you ever wondered how someone can serve in the church, and still not be healed? Have you ever asked God questions like this? I know if you asked why, he would tell you what he told me. Forgive! Be transparent! Don't die in your wilderness. He told me, "Yes, you have to forgive the ones who took your son. You have to forgive your aunt. Yes, you have to forgive everyone that was involved." Oh, and guess what else. He said, "You have to forgive yourself."

I really thought I could never live again! I wondered what God was doing. I wondered why every time I came into the church I got this feeling like I was in the clouds with my son looking at me, but then my eyes would begin to water and the tears would start again. I would sit in church thinking about all the pain, sorrow, and sadness that this situation had inflicted on my life. But one day, the Lord began to speak to my spirit woman and tell me that it was going to be okay. I heard God clearly and he told me that he was going to bring me all the way out this time. Healing was my portion, but I needed to forgive first. The Lord directed me to write each name on a piece of paper and mark them off after I had forgiven them. As I sat in church on that Sunday morning, I struggled with hurt, disappointment, and hate for everyone, but God saw my pain and knew the root was coming from my son's death, hurt from my previous marriage, my family, and even the pain I inflicted on myself. My pastor at the time could see that I was struggling with my situation, but I thought, "I can't cry. Not today. I might not be able to stop." I wondered if I could get through the service without acting a fool, because I was reliving every situation that had ever caused me pain.

On Mother's Day, in the middle of the church floor, I realized that if I was going to truly live for God and do his will, I had to face my biggest demons. God began to heal me inside out. I was tired, frustrated, and depression had taken over my life. I thank God for using my pastor on that day to give me the time and the space to cry and spend time in the heavenly realm of God. This was a feeling that I had never experienced before; God took me to a place where he ministered to my spirit and allowed me to see that my son was in a good place. I realize now that he lived out his own destiny. You never know who God will use to bring healing and deliverance to you. But there, in the middle of the floor, He used my pastor to usher me into a place I could have never reached alone. Sometimes we need sincere people in our lives that care about our spiritual wellbeing. After that service, I knew that I could live again.

After that service, it was time for me to put into motion the process of forgiving and to begin to heal. The first person I needed to forgive was my cousin, who had suffered a massive stroke just one week after my revelation, and was in the ICU. I remember that when I received the call about his condition, all I could think about is that if he was going to die, I wanted him to go knowing that I forgave him. On my trip to the hospital I cried and asked God for forgiveness for living so long with this hatred in my heart. But when I walked into his room he had just died. This taught me to forgive quickly because you don't know how long people are going to be a part of your life. This situation threw me for a loop, but I could not let it keep me from moving forward in my spiritual walk. My prayer life increased and I begin to read the Word more. I began to rebuild my relationship with my aunt and I forgave her for whatever part I felt she had played in the death of my son. After forgiving my family and forgiving the people who shot my son, I was able to go back to the place where he was shot. My first time there, as I walked up to the area, I felt God moving and healing my broken heart. I needed to go for my own closure.

The next step I had to take, was to forgive my ex-husband and also his wife. I was mad with him because I felt like he did not build a relationship with his children and that his wife was somehow complicit. I blamed him for things over which he had absolutely no control. But the Lord said forgive! I asked God to help me to forgive sincerely and not to allow the situation to have control over my life. So as God ministered to my spirit woman, I was able to forgive and reach out, not knowing what the results would be. All I knew is that this needed to happen for me to move forward. Today, I declare victory in Jesus. I realized from this situation all things are possible with God.

After I reaching a state of forgiveness, it was time for me to give back and allow people to see what the Lord had done in my life. I started reaching out to other mothers who had lost children to violence to see if I could be a witness to them. In doing this, I realized that my assignment in God was bigger and that God was preparing me for a restoration ministry to women who left God because of their own wilderness experiences. Look at God! Your pain is bigger than you! I know my pain was bigger than me.

Initially, I thought that my assignment was only for mothers who lost children to violence, but do you know God is bigger than one demographic? What he began allowing me to see, was that my assignment was multifold and I would help to restore woman back to God after *any* event that caused them to walk away from our savior. Though this experience, I learned that my relationship with the Lord needed to be grounded because people who left God due to traumatic events would not easily come back. If you are reading my story, my question to you is, did that issue or situation that you are facing cause you to walk away from our savior because you felt like he didn't fix it the way you thought he should? Please don't think or allow anyone to tell you that they didn't feel the same way.

When I look back at the four years prior to me writing my story, I know that it's time to hit the ground running and pursing the road God laid out for me. Through my prayers, God was securing in me my assignment and the plans for my journey. The one scripture I must quote is Jeremiah 29:11 from the King James Bible: "For I know the thoughts that I think toward you, saith the Lord, thoughts of peace, and not of evil, to give you an expected end." I needed the Lord to allow this scripture to rest in my heart, because the enemy was trying to stop what God had put in motion. The Lord was allowing me to give my testimony to many so that the wounded would find me; this was God's doing, not my own. Through all of this I realize that prayer was most important in my healing and development into the woman God has ordained. I know that it is because of my prayer life with God that I am who I am today. The Lord has developed my prayer life into a strong force with which the Devil cannot compete. I know today that if it had not been for prayer, I would have lost my mind a long time ago.

I now reflect on my son's death with different eyes. I know that the Lord used this tragic event to set me in alignment. I want you to know that my Savior takes any situation or disaster to get you where he needs you to be. My destiny was determined in my mother's womb and I'm glad to now be in alignment with the master plan.

I have learned that forgiveness and prayer is the answer to most of our problems. I know it was the answer for mine. The Lord gave me what I needed in this season to impact others who suffer and walk away from God and the church. As a senior pastor, I realize that my journey brought me to the road I'm traveling now. Today, I use what I lost to impact a nation of people who have lost their way. I submit to helping others find their potential in God and pushing them to live out their assignment. Can you see how God had his hand in the plan? I know that his hand is in any plan or situation you are facing. Just know that God will turn your tragedy into victory, and your pain into your passion. You can live again, no matter what situation or circumstances you face, if you submit to God's plan and will for your life.

Chapter 4

Transforming from Ladybug to God's Lady

Lady Tawanda Holmes

The Ladybug Is Lost

My paternal grandmother fondly called me Lady, short for ladybug. She died in 1999 and I never asked her why she gave me that nickname. There were times when I didn't feel worthy of the name, but it made me feel special and loved since a ladybug was so beautiful. She gave birth to 13 children but loss 2 during birth. My father was the oldest and I'm second to the oldest grandchild. She moved from Emporia, Virginia to Baltimore, Maryland with her husband before age 20. My grandfather owned a carpentry business and my grandmother was a homemaker. When most of the children were grown and out of the house, my grandparents split. I don't know why since I only visited on weekends.

My grandmother earned her GED at the age of 55 and pursued a career in nursing. She worked 12-hour shifts. Knowing this is one of reasons I'm so driven. She was absolutely beautiful in her white uniform, popping her mints to ensure she had fresh breath, wearing her Charlie perfume and heading to the bus stop to go to work. She never drove. I guess I was about 10 when I started taking the bus alone to visit her. I would get off and walk across the street to approach my grandmother's house, which was only a block away. My cousins would come running toward me yelling, "Wanda is here," and hugging me. It was awesome. While my grandmother was working, my aunts kept the house cleaned, cooked dinner, played loud music—Rick James, Hall and Oates—and smoked weed. They were only 10-12 years older than me and they lived there with their children. It was a five-bedroom, three-story house in West Baltimore with a porch to hang out with friends playing games, talking, laughing, and dancing. I loved that house and my family. I lost my virginity in that house under the age of 18.

I lived with my mother in Lafayette projects in East Baltimore. It was pretty nice when we first got there in 1975. I was only five at the time, and I lived there with my mother, younger brother, and my stepfather. It was a two-bedroom apartment on the seventh floor in one of the five high-rise buildings. Although we were poor, we had some good times. My mother didn't work. She had dropped out of high school to have me at the age of 18. My father, the handsome, smooth ladies' man played no part in raising me. He was only 19 and he didn't finish school either. He served a little time in jail and became a Muslim, but once he came home, he was back to running women and drinking. He sometimes worked with my grandfather and I would occasionally see him at my grandmother's house. He either lived with her, some woman, or his sister. I actually didn't have any ill feelings toward him and enjoyed the small conversations we had. I just wished he didn't drink so much. When I was 11, he tried to insinuate that my great uncle (grandmother's brother) could be my father. I never asked my mother or my uncle who, in hindsight, always hugged me tight whenever he saw me. I never understood why until my father made the comment to me. To this day, I still wonder.

The Ladybug Is Crushed

My father never came to visit me. He claimed it was because of my stepfather. So, I called my brother's father daddy since he helped my mother take care of me. He was also a handsome light-skinned man like my father. I guess that was my mother's type. She was dark-skinned, thin, and pretty. She would sometimes disappear for days and we would not know where she went. That's when my brother's father began touching me while I was sleeping. As I got older, I learned she was sneaking around with other men and my father was one of them. When she came home, he would beat her and one time, gave her a concussion. During one of their fights, I thought it was the appropriate time to tell her what he was doing to me. While they were outside cussing at each other, I whispered to my little brother to tell mommy that daddy was touching me while she was gone. So, he went to the door and screamed it out and the cussing stopped. My mother was shocked and my brother's father ran off to his parents' house who lived about three miles away. My mother called the police; they took a report and took me to the hospital.

    I was only seven years old and I had to learn new words like vagina instead of "down there." It was difficult to describe what happened in court in front of everyone. Ironically enough, my father and grandfather were painting a courtroom several doors down from the courtroom where we were. I remember catching a cramp in my neck from laying my head in my mother's lap with my head turned away from my brother's father, sitting about 10 feet away from us in the hallway as we waited for our case to be called. He was convicted and served time in jail. My mother's relationship with his parents changed after that. They fussed at her for leaving me with him.

My maternal grandmother had mental issues, so I know it hurt to lose the relationship she had with his parents. After the ordeal, the children in my neighborhood teased me about being molested, saying cruel things like I needed maxi pads, though I didn't even know what they were. My mother and I were different too, and I felt unloved and humiliated.

Check day, the day when all the mothers would get their welfare checks, was the first of the month. We would go to Old Town Mall to shop and eat at the food stands. On those days, everyone was in a good mood: loud talking, laughing, and dancing. We would run into my cousin and her mother (my mother's oldest sister), and my best friend and her mother while shopping. My cousin and my best friend lived in the same building as I did and they both lived on the first floor. We were all close and had some great times together. My best friend's house was the party house. People were in and out all day and night: drinking, playing music, and talking. My cousin and I liked hanging out there. My mother met her new boyfriend at my best friend's house. He was my best friend's uncle and same type as the other men she had dated. He moved in with us and my mother had another baby boy by him. At the time, I was 9 and my other brother was 6. Although there were some great times in the projects, it was still a dark place of drugs, shootings, and prostitution.

I was always a good student, but I only had a few friends. I was also teased about my maternal grandmother, who was the neighborhood crazy lady and lived in the projects two miles away. She would cuss folks out for just walking by, moon them, and whatever else came to mind at the moment. She was a heavy drinker too. She was mentally ill, the effects of which carried over to all of her daughters (including my mother) except one, my oldest aunt. Although she was a teen mom and lived in the projects too, she eventually went back to school, got her nursing degree, a career and moved out of the projects. She had a beautiful home in west Baltimore, got married, and had three cars. We loved visiting her.

The Ladybug Is Confused

Instead of going to my zoned school, I attended Western High School, the oldest all girl public school in the country, which was known for having students who excelled in academics and athletics. At this school everyone was smart. Some of the girls who started there with me were not there after the first year because the work was too intense. The school was across town, and catching the bus so far away gave me an incentive to sneak off or delay me coming home. I cannot tell you why I was so rebellious. I guess it was hormonal. My mother threatened to transfer me to the school that was zoned for my neighborhood. She took me to a counselor and the counselor helped me get a summer job as a day camp advisor, which helped somewhat. I was 14. At the summer job, my supervisor was a grad student from DC. She was 23 and amazing. She talked to me about dressing appropriately, like the fact that I should wear black under white clothes because otherwise my undergarments would show. She took me and two other team members to Towsontown mall. It's less than 10 miles from my apartment, but I had never been. We mostly looked around and she took us to a restaurant. She showed us how to place our napkins in our laps and she paid using her American Express, which I had never seen before. She worked another part time job as a waitress at a restaurant at the Inner Harbor. After the summer job was over, she got me a job in the ice cream section of the restaurant. That job changed my life because I was too busy making money and going to school to be mischievous.

I was working with teens from all over the city who attended different schools (public and private) and various income levels. This was also the culture of my high school, which exposed me to various perspectives. We had so much fun at work, and that was where I met my new best friend. She was a year ahead of me at our school and lived in West Baltimore. I had to distance myself from the other friend who was very smart, but stopped going to school around 8th grade. My new best friend and I were always going shopping and going to the movies. Although she graduated a year before me and eventually found another job, we remained close until age 35, when life took us on different paths.

After I graduated from high school, I got a job at Social Security Administration downtown. One of my classmates started the same day too. You could not tell us anything. We had federal government jobs, making $5.77 an hour when minimum wage was $3.35. Her father was a pastor. She was so sweet, the opposite of me. I had become abrasive, impatient, and vindictive. I didn't really know how to have a healthy relationship with other women since my mother and I were not close. I don't know why the pastor's daughter and I clicked. Maybe she saw a witnessing opportunity. My mother took us to church maybe once a year. There was the Good News Club, a Bible Study for children in our neighborhood when I was around 9 or 10. I learned John 3:16: For God so loved the world that he gave his only begotten Son, that whosoever believeth in him should not perish but have everlasting life.

I managed to get my own one bedroom apartment and my classmate moved my things in her car one week after my 18th birthday. She owned a car since the age of 16. After one year, I got a promotion to a position in Baltimore County working Fridays through Tuesday 2pm–10:30pm. It was an ugly shift, but I was single and didn't have any children. It kept me out of trouble since my love life was in shambles. I did, however, manage to become involved with a married man in which I was totally clueless to his status. I also allowed another guy to move into my apartment. After a short while, he became physically abusive and during an argument, he choked me until I passed out. That was my wake up call to get out of that relationship.

Working the night shift allowed me to go back to school. I had always wanted to go to college, and while dating a guy on my job who was a student at Morgan state, he brought me the application and I enrolled. All was well until we were breaking up. Seeing him in school and work was too much, so I did something drastic and enlisted in the navy reserves. Boot camp was eight weeks in Orlando FL. I still have all of the letters sent to me while I was there. My job had to hold my position for me until I returned and I only missed one semester of school. When I returned, I got engaged to a middle school teacher who had a daughter in Pennsylvania. He was a nice guy, but I was not the best wife. I should have waited until I graduated to get married. Instead, I worked a full-time job, attended school full-time and had navy reserve duty one weekend a month and two weeks a year. To make matters worse, after I graduated, I took a position with the Department of Energy, requiring me to audit utility companies in a 100 percent travel status. I rationalized it by telling myself I was doing it for us, not realizing the godly principles of marriage and making him a priority. I stayed on the road for nine months and came home every other weekend. I was reassigned to the DC office and gave birth to our son two years later. I stayed after his first affair. After the third, I filed for divorce.

Though it ended, two great things happened to me during this marriage: having my son and finding my first church home. My son melted my heart and was the sweetest baby. My first church was apostolic and I loved the members, my pastor and his wife. I learned the importance of salvation and how to have a relationship with Christ. I learned about giving and discovered my spiritual gifts along the way. I also learned how to be a servant leader and how to have healthy relationships with other women. I became really close to one of the sisters at the church. She worked for radiation oncology and I admired how she talked to the patients. It was years later that she became a two-time breast and colon cancer survivor. I am blessed to know her. I thank God for the pastor and his wife for pouring so much into me. My ex-husband and I had joint custody, taking care of our son on alternate weeks. At the time, I was taking grad classes, studying for the CPA exam, still working with the federal government, teaching at a community college and still in the navy reserves. It was the perfect time to be single. I also cleaned up my credit and bought a single-family house for me and my son. I had no idea credit was a big deal until mine was ruined. I was transitioning into God's lady.

My cousin gave me the number of a guy I dated years ago. I called and we talked for hours. He was a deacon at his church and eight years older than me. It was so nice to talk to a saved man. On our first date, he said, "I'm going to marry you." I thought, yeah okay. I definitely wanted to remarry, but I didn't more children. He had two teenagers from a previous marriage, but he wanted one more child. He decided it was not a deal breaker for him that I didn't want more children, and we started spending a lot of time together, attending family gatherings and visiting each other's churches. I wanted to make sure he didn't have any other women. We got engaged and had premarital counseling with my pastor and his wife. It was really nice to hear a husband and a wife's perspective. After we got married, we both left our churches and joined a different church. It was so hard to leave my church, but I knew my husband and I needed to be at the same church. My husband and the pastor of our new church were good friends. The church was so friendly. Then, my husband dropped a bomb. He told me that he was called to preach the Gospel. I wasn't ready to be a minister's wife. However, I was very proud of him for obtaining his license.

On top of this, I had my own shocking revelation. I was hospitalized with a blood clot in my lung. At the time, they thought it was a side effect of the birth control pills I was taking, so I stopped using them. As a result, I got pregnant twice, giving birth to our two sons 17 months apart. I guess my husband had his prayers answered twice.

Our life seemed to be in constant transition, as another major change occurred. A pastor at another church was sick and was considering retirement. He asked my husband to come and study under him to become the next pastor of his church. I was just learning to embrace my role as a minister's wife and now I would have to prepare to be a pastor's wife. My pastor's wife and I attended a pastor/minister's wives conference in Texas. It was an awesome experience, and I was able to meet other pastor's wives from Baltimore. The conference inspired me to begin asking around about whether a conference or some type of mentoring or classes were being held in Baltimore. The other pastors' wives mentioned there were some meetings in Baltimore, but no one knew the location of the meetings and there were no websites. This was in 2010. I began taking classes at the Baltimore School of the Bible because I wanted to be an effective pastor's wife. After 18 years in the navy reserves, I didn't reenlist. It was one of the most difficult decisions I ever had to make. My goal was to reach 20 years so I could retire. But if I had stayed, I would have been deployed to either Iraq or Afghanistan for 6 months. It was no big deal to me. However, my children were 3, 4, and 13 and there was a family intervention. So, I decided not to reenlist. My stepdaughter was also living with us since her mother died of breast cancer. She was about 16 and was a great help to us. I just adored the relationship she had with my husband. My husband accepted the position as the assistant pastor at the new church. So, my mother-in-law, our children, and I served faithfully. We had the opportunity to lead various ministries. It was nice to serve with my mother-in-law. I was glad we were able to move past our differences and establish a good relationship. I can talk to her about anything except her son, but I'm okay with that. We stayed at this church five years until my husband accepted the position as the pastor at our current church. We are so grateful that God sent us to this loving church and our children are serving faithfully with us.

Transformed to God's Lady

I have come to realize that all of my experiences helped me to get to this place. This is my story of how the Lord has carried me through some difficult situations: from poverty, molestation, an abusive relationship, a failed marriage, and an almost fatal illness. These trials allowed me to experience God's grace, mercy, and agape love. Romans 8:28 (NIV) says, "And we know that in all things God works for the good of those who love him, who have been called according to his purpose." I thank God for the people He placed in my life to mentor and encourage me. My experiences led me to gather other ministers/pastors' wives to start a non-profit to mentor minister and pastors' wives and provide community service. These are some awesome women. I also founded another group of first ladies. We call ourselves CC's girls. They have blessed me tremendously with their wisdom. I have a heart for women and a desire to empower them. My prayer is that my story encourages you and that you find Him faithful as He has been to me. If He saved and made provisions for me, He is able to do it for anyone. God does all things well. I thank God for transforming me into His lady.

Chapter 5

Life on Earth Is Preparation for Glory

Michelle Baylor

So, whether you eat or drink, or whatever you do, do all to the glory of God.

—*1 Corinthians 10:31 ESV*

What is the meaning of life? God created the first human beings, Adam and Eve, in the Garden of Eden where He gave them life and a purpose in life. God put them in charge of all the animals (Genesis 1) and they were to take care of the Garden of Eden (Genesis 2). Just like our fore parents, Adam and Eve, our purpose in life is to take care of ourselves, other people, and the land God made.

As Billy Graham stated, "Everything that happens prior to death is a preparation for the journey" (Billy Graham, BGEA Decision Magazine, January, 2015).

Life begins the moment we are conceived. God knows each of us before our conception and throughout our physical lives, and He knows our destination in eternity. Everything we do in life is preparing us for our final destination after our physical bodies cease to breath and dies. The question each of us must ask ourselves is, "Where will I spend eternity?" My final eternal destination is heaven. As a believer, a Born Again Daughter of Zion (BADZ), I will be absent from my body and present with the Lord (2 Corinthians 5:8).

The story of my life as preparation for heaven is full of both good and not so good times. The great part is that I have a direct and eternal connection to Jesus. This connection supplies me with the spiritual strength and power to withstand all of the events in my life that are good and not so good. God does not let us know the exact day and time our physical life will end, but we do know it will end. Our physical life is not just for our personal gain alone, but to affect those with whom we engage. One of my favorite sermons is "The Drum Major Instinct," by Dr. Martin Luther King, Jr. which is from a 1952 homily by J. Wallace Hamilton entitled "Drum-Major Instincts" (*Ride the Wild Horses!*). Dr. King preached this sermon from the pulpit of Ebenezer Baptist Church in

Atlanta, Georgia. He gave his desired eulogy in the last portion of his Drum Major Instinct sermon on February 4, 1968, two months before his assassination on April 4, 1968. The first portion of the sermon addresses the response of Jesus to his disciples, James and John, the sons of Zebedee who wanted to have a place of prominence in the new kingdom Jesus would establish (Mark 10:35). At the end of the sermon, Dr. King talks about his own death, what he leaves behind, and how he wants to be remembered. Dr. King said he just wanted to "leave a committed life behind." He spoke from the song *If I can Help Somebody* by Alma Bazel Androzzo written in 1945 for the National Tuberculosis Society (Alma Bazel Androzzo/Boosey And Hawkes Inc/ASCAP). Dr King spoke in part, "If I can help somebody as I pass along…If I can spread the message as the master taught, then my living will not be in vain." I believe Dr. King wanted to emphasize the fact that God gives us life to glorify Him and bless others.

It is good to look back and reflect on the life that God has allowed us to live. My story has similarities to the story of many but it is unique to me in its details. I have overcome the challenges of insecurity, grief, divorce, and abuse, both mental and emotional. Each time I am knocked down, it is God who keeps me from being knocked out completely. The Apostle Paul says we are "Persecuted, but not forsaken; cast down, but not destroyed" (2 Corinthians 4:9). There have been times when I really felt like giving up and just walking around feeling sorry for myself. God, the "lifter of my head" (Psalm 3:3), has given and continues to give me the strength to fight the battles in my life.

My twin brother, Mike, and I were raised in a Christian home where our parents insisted that going to church and Sunday school was not an option. At the age of 9, our parents separated and my dad moved out. However, my dad made sure we did not feel abandoned or feel the stigma of his not physically living in our home. In the 1950's, within the circles I traveled, single-parent homes were small in number. Dad took us to school every day and when he could not make it because of his profession, our uncle who lived nearby, took us to school. Dad continued to provide a home for us and was continuously involved in our schooling. Dad lived less than one mile from us so that if his presence was needed at our house, he was there in a matter of minutes. I never say Mike and I were from a "broken home." What we had was an extended home because we spent quite a bit of time at our dad's house. Our birth mom never talked negatively about our dad around Mike and I, and she always encouraged us to spend time with him. She loved her twins dearly and wanted us to be happy and have fulfilled lives.

Dad took us on vacations and several short trips and events throughout the year. I still vividly remember our great vacations in Wildwood and Atlantic City, New

Jersey, the World's Fair and Coney Island in New York, Montreal and Quebec, Canada, me in Spain, Mike in Hawaii, and the list goes on. I cannot forget the many trips and church homecomings Dad took us to in his hometown, King William, Virginia.

Dad lived a Godly, upright life and did not date excessively. One day he introduced Mike and me to a lovely lady he was dating and allowed us to spend quite a bit of time with her. Dad and this lovely lady were in love and in 1969 they got married. Mike and I were 18 and both of us were in the wedding of our dad and our wonderful, loving second mom, who used the term "second mom." She sincerely loved us and never tried to replace, but only supplement our first mom. All the good things I have learned about being a second mom, I learned from my second mom. She loved our dad very much and lived out her marriage vows to be with him in sickness and in health. She stayed by his side until the day he died.

During my childhood and into my teens, I was rather unrefined and awkward. My first mom and grandmother tried to teach me how to act like a "lady" from an early age. However, at the age of 15, I was still unrefined. Mom sent me to the Patricia Stevens Modeling School, a charm school in Baltimore, Maryland, to build my confidence and learn the social graces. The charm school attempted to teach me how to walk, dress, put on makeup, stand, sit, eat properly with proper place settings, and the art of social conversation. I learned a lot but never liked the style of wearing gloves and a hat when I was not cold.

Growing up I was an introvert, very shy and a bookworm. Boys did not ask me out, but having a twin brother proved very helpful. My brother got me a date for my junior prom and years later, my brother had a buddy who became my first husband. After high school I went to college for two months, dropped out of school and started working at the Social Security Administration (SSA) at the age of 18. I came out of my shell, started drinking heavily, partied 7 days a week, and dropped out of church. Within three years' time, my lifestyle was ungodly and the complete opposite of what my parents and grandparents tried to teach me.

The Vietnam War was hot and heavy during this time in the late 60's and early 70's. My boyfriend, who later became husband number one, joined the United States Marines. He went to Vietnam in 1968 during the heavy fighting of the Tet Offensive. The uncertainty of war changed greatly how our society lived at that time. While many were on their knees praying without ceasing, I was in the bar drinking incessantly.

My first husband and I separated early in our marriage. The next major change in my life occurred when after 11 years, 2 months, and 15 days of working at SSA, I joined the United States Army. I spent the first 2 years in the Army reserves as a truck driver. I then went on active duty for 8 years in the field of Military Intelligence, which proved to be one of my best jobs. I loved the very interesting work and the regimented Army life. But even at this point, I continued to drink and party heavily which is very easy to do in the military. I was "out there," but I am blessed to say that I did not stay "out there."

While in the Army my involvement in church and chapel activities gradually increased and the chapel became my place of comfort and joy. In 1985, I was stationed in South Korea and began spending a lot of time alone in my room. This is where God spoke to my heart, telling me to change my life to one that honors Him. I listened, committed my life to Jesus and began a real personal relationship with Him. I felt then, and I continue to feel, the peace of God in my heart. Paul writes in Philippians 4:7 (KJV), "And the peace of God, which passeth all understanding, shall keep your hearts and minds through Christ Jesus." This peace of God cannot be fully defined by man. It is a peace that only God can provide. As a child, the priest at the church I attended always quoted this scripture as part of his benediction. It was not until I surrendered my heart to the Lord that I understood the profundity and blessing of this scripture. Every time I hear, read, or quote this scripture my heart is soothed by the peace of God.

Although a person gives his life to Jesus, the journey of life is not always smooth and uneventful. The most difficult time I have ever experienced in my life was when I had to bury my twin brother Mike. During this time, our family mortician, a brother-in-Christ, served and ministered greatly to me through his calling from God. More importantly, it was the Christ in our mortician that comforted me at a time when I could not see Christ clearly. About two weeks after my twin passed in 2003, I was hit with deep grief that had me bound so deeply I could not pray. I could not stop crying! A very important part of me was gone—my twin, my confidant, and my best friend. The blessing is that Mike was saved and is now in heaven waiting for the heavenly arrival of his saved loved ones and friends. My first birthday after the death of Mike was a very heavy, dark, and depressing day for me. Our birthday had always been a very special day to us and we cherished dearly the day we were born together. I often teased Mike about being his big sister. I was born 15 ½ minutes before him.

My medical doctor recognized the depth of my grief. Because of my deep faith in God my doctor felt I did not need medication, but she highly recommended grief counseling. I attended six sessions with a grief counselor who mentioned Jesus during our first session and from that point on our sessions were very blessed and beneficial. At the beginning of each session she put a box of tissues in front of me as I talked and cried. One day while I was alone in the midst of my deep grief and constant crying I asked God, "Why did you take *my* brother?" The Holy Spirit spoke to my heart and said, "He was not yours." I thought, wow! My intellect was supposed to know that, but because the hole in my heart was so big and the pain so great, I could not think positively. God had to speak to me through that consuming pain. I was immediately released from the grief that had me bound. This was my watershed moment, which revealed to me that our loved ones are only loaned to us on earth but our love for them never dies. At that moment I thanked and praised God for the 53 years He allowed Mike and me to share on this side of eternity. I apologized to God and thanked Him for removing the scales from my eyes and my heart that kept me from seeing Him while I grieved. I now rejoice when I talk and think about my twin, our life together, and our many escapades. I miss him and there are times when I cry thinking about him.

I was blessed to retire three years before my twin died. Years later, when my father and two mothers died, I had the opportunity to spend ample end of lifetime with all of them while doing what needed to be done during their illnesses. I am really blessed to have loving memories of all of the times spent in their homes, hospitals, doctors' offices, rehabilitation facilities, and long-term care facilities. Grief is something I will never completely get over but, praise God, it is now well managed.

God uses our pain and His blessings to minister to others by sharing our stories. Sometime after my twin died, the twin of one of my neighbors died. As I approached her house to visit, I saw my neighbor walking in the middle of the street in a daze. I was able to embrace and cry with her because we both knew the pain losing a twin. Another incident occurred during the time my dad was in a long-term care facility, very close to death and nonresponsive. I sat by his bed daily. One day a nursing assistant working in the facility asked me how I was able to calmly sit during this time. She asked, "How do you do this?" I told her that my dad was saved and would soon be in heaven, and that is what comforted me. I knew Dad would be in heaven with Jesus waiting for the rest of us saved ones. Because of that conversation, I was able to lead the nursing assistant to the Lord that day. She is now a believer and has a place in heaven throughout eternity!

Mike passed in September of 2003; dad passed in September of 2007; mom number two passed one year and ten months later in July, 2009, and mom number one passed in December, 2016. Although my earthly family is dwindling physically, I have an ever-increasing spiritual family. I rest in the comfort of the everlasting arms of God. God says in Jeremiah 31:25 (KJV), "For I have satiated the weary soul, and I have replenished every sorrowful soul."

I was married to husband number two for seven years when our marriage ended and my life changed drastically. My finances took a serious nosedive and because my bills had to be paid, I was unable to pay my tithes for three months. I went to an attorney for legal advice and he told me that although he did not know me very well, he knew my tithes were taken care of by my non-monetary contributions. One of my dearest friends and true sister-in-Christ, whom God brought into my life about 20 years ago, told me I would be alright because I was a good steward of my resources. These two individuals were very comforting and their encouragement kept me from going into a place of deep despair. Neither of them knew at the time the impact of their encouraging words. How many of us have had someone to speak into our lives the very words we need to hear? Only God can orchestrate those life-changing conversations.

I seek God for guidance and comfort through each bump in the road of my life. God's Holy Spirit has and continues to guide, comfort, and teach me the purposes of my life experiences. I also continue to praise and worship God in those good and not so good times. I love the story of Job, which is a great lesson on the faithfulness of God to his faithful, no matter what happens. Job worshipped God in the midst of his worse troubles and loss (Job 1:20). God restored and gave Job double what he had before (Job 42:10).

I have learned to forgive because the Word of God commands it. Forgiveness frees those of us who have been wronged and eliminates any resulting bitterness that can take root and grow in our hearts (Hebrews 12:15). I have had to truly forgive in my heart in order to be free (John 8:36, Galatians 5:1). God cannot use me for His glory if I harbor anger toward a person who is a sinner like me; I can only pray for them. I also have learned how to be humble and ask for forgiveness of sin from God and those I have wronged. When we confess our sins, our loving God is "faithful and just to forgive us *our* sins and to cleanse us from all unrighteousness" (1 John 1:9 KJV). This confession of sin must be more than lip service; it must come from the heart.

There have been times I was tempted and did take matters into my own hands because of the many attacks I suffered. These attacks were in the forms of envy, hurt, deception, attempted demonic manipulations (strong spiritual warfare), attempted financial ruin, character assassination, and attempted human control. I have and continue to overcome attacks by prayer and the guidance and counsel of God the Holy Spirit who lives in me. I have learned that I cannot successfully repay evil deeds done to me. The battle belongs to God (2 Chronicles 20:15), and He will fight for those of us who belong to Him.

My daily prayer is for the Holy Spirit to show more of Jesus through me. I pray that as He fills me daily, less of Michelle and more of Jesus will show. Reading and studying the Word of God is truly beneficial and a must for me. I am able to hide the Word in my heart (Psalm 119:11, Deuteronomy 11:18) from which to pull and apply to my life. Although I do not always remember the exact words, I do know the biblical principles by which I am to live. God tells me in His Word to confess, praise, petition, and thank Him during my earthly journey until my destination is reached in heaven, face to face with Jesus.

The more time I spend in the presence of the Lord, the stronger my spiritual muscle. Ephesians 6:10 (KJV) says, "Finally, my brethren, be strong in the Lord, and in the power of his might." Life experiences and challenges can put us in bondage but the Spirit of God in us can free us from the long-term effects of that bondage. This is a bondage that can imprison our minds and thereby affect our spiritual, physical, and emotional wellbeing. So, I became a fitness enthusiast and I work out 5 – 6 days a week. My exercise and strength training are building my physical, mental, and emotional muscles.

My prayer is that all who read my story and all whose lives cross my path are blessed by the God inspired testimony of my life, a Born Again Daughter of Zion (BADZ). More importantly, I pray that the Holy Spirit will prick hearts and lead individuals to a personal relationship with Jesus Christ, God the Son. It does not matter what you have done because "all have sinned, and come short of the Glory of God" (Romans 3:23 KJV). But when you confess your sins, believe that God raised Jesus from the dead, and make Jesus the LORD of your life, you are saved and have a place in eternity with God, Jesus, and the Holy Spirit (Romans 10:9). Peace and Blessings to all!

Chapter 6

"IT"

Arvinese I. Reid

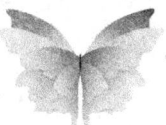

It happened; you went through it;
you can recover from it.

The word "it" is used to represent an inanimate thing, understood as something previously mentioned, about to be mentioned, or present in the immediate context. At one time or another, "it" happened to you. You couldn't explain "it." You could not believe "it," and in some instances you did not know your "it" was even happening. Still, you went through "it." Your "it" is any experience in which the Devil of your soul would have loved for you to lose your mind—periods of months or years of your life that you thought you lost while you were in "it," and hours of sleep you lost wondering if you were going to make it through "it." Your "it" is that pivotal, life altering event that if left up to Satan, you would not have lived through to read this book.

My "it" took place over a period of years, and came to a crucial point when I asked myself, can I do this for another 10 years? During my "it," I was merely existing day to day, coping with deceit, betrayal, adultery, denial, shame, guilt, and low self-esteem. If you found any of your "it" in that list as you read, I want you to know you can recover. Our "it" may be different, and I may not know the degree of what you suffered, but what I do know and have been sent to tell you is that you can recover and be restored to a place of wholeness, a place that is even better than you were before. Isn't that just like Jesus? He said in Ephesians 3:20 (NKJV), "Now to him who is able to do exceedingly abundantly above all that we ask or think, according to the power that works in us."

My "it" was necessary for me to be a living testimony, and to be able to tell you that you can recover and live in the fullness of Jesus. My relationship with Jesus, keeping it real with him and the vessels that he orchestrated to heal through His word, gave me a forgiving heart so that I can say, yes, "it" happened; yes, I went through "it;" yes, I can recover from "it;" yes, I am healed and whole in the name of Jesus.

My "it" began in 2006. I was thirty-four years old when I married the man who asked for my hand in marriage after a year of dating. The courting stage was fun; friendship and partnership were fostered. The wedding was picturesque and the reception was grand. I was a single mother when I got married so this was a joyous occasion, especially having been told that no one would marry a woman that already had a child. I was excited to defy the odds—maybe a little too excited.

Thinking back to the dating process, I realize there were a few "red flags" that I may have ignored or been blind to because of the pretty bling on my finger. Maybe the idea of being married and having the husband that we read about, or that help meet that the word of God tells us about, was just so enticing that I got sidetracked, pulled away from the practical, realistic questions that we should all ask when dating. The idea of being married in ministry to another person that loved the Lord like me was amazing. And it was great for our pastor at the time; she had these two mature servants that loved God, ready to get married and continue in ministry. But the more realistic notion that just serving God together is not all that we needed to know about each other became a big reality. After approximately three years of marriage, I began noticing things like strange websites on the computer that were brushed off as pop-ups, like maybe we had been hacked and gay pornography just appeared. There was also the excuse that he had browsed the websites out of mere curiosity. I also noticed a lot of behaviors that were not conducive to a productive marriage. The obvious was becoming apparent. I was not the object of my spouse's affection and my marriage was in trouble. Discussions about the topic were often dismissed and he blamed me for it. Since I worked two jobs to make ends meet, he made the excuse that I was too busy for us to spend time together and work on our relationship.

As the years went by, there were no kick and scream arguments, no door slamming, and we were always cordial—the best of platonic friends. On the inside, I knew that the love was not there as a husband should love a wife, or like the love that we read about in Ephesians 5:25. But I was also aware that the direction in Ephesians 5:22 that states, "Wives submit to your own husbands, as to the Lord," was a heavy load of trust that I did not have for the man that I married. I could not pinpoint why or I chose not to acknowledge why at that time. Don't get me wrong, we cared for each other and I fulfilled the "in sickness and health" part. The relationship was amicable and the duties were performed according to the Word of God, but the heart was missing from the equation.

Ministry was a high point in my marriage, as I was a youth pastor and a minister, and serving under a seasoned leader, there was always work in the kingdom to do. My husband served as a trustee, among other church duties. Our conversations were most exciting when we talked church. That was our common interest instead of the heartfelt connection that a husband and wife should share. There were many ministry successes that we were used for by God and his mercy. Families were blessed, young people were taught the ways of the Lord and taught how to pray and build effective relationships with Jesus Christ. Couples looked at us and said they wanted what we had. But I was using ministry as anesthesia, instead of dealing with the betrayal, hurt, and even adultery. The joy that I got seeing how God would move through me in the lives of his people became more important to me than my own issues and feelings. I felt my worth in service of any capacity, even in driving the church van to transport the people of God. But my heart was broken and my "it" was escalating. I cried out to God in my prayer time and asked him to reveal what was really happening and what was wrong in my marriage.

Please receive this disclaimer into your spirit: when you ask God to reveal anything to you and he does, be ready, because a flowery bed of roses will not always be what is shown to you. More things were revealed through dreams, visions, and seeing obvious things such as texts and web sites that screamed affair. A separation had been discussed a couple of years prior, but I was not ready to face or come to terms with "it." This was the Devil, I thought. I am a minister of the Gospel; I can't be separated or divorced. What would people say? How would I explain this to people the people that I ministered to, prayed with and even gave marriage advice to? These are the things I would say to myself and the conversations that I would have with God.

I continued to allow myself to receive less than what Jesus had intended for me in marriage. After he told me "I love you, but I'm not in love with you," our communication changed, and we only discussed what was necessary. There was no enjoyable conversation or even laughter. I did not feel that I could ever be vulnerable; I always had to be strong. I did not feel protected morally, emotionally, or physically because I knew he was living a secret life.

I felt myself shutting down to family and friends and immersing myself into work and ministry. I was determined to be the "woman of God" that I was called to be. Even if I was dying on the inside, I would not disappoint Jesus or let the work that He charged to my hand, fall to the ground. I would shower in tears, drive in tears, and ask the Lord where the love was that I read about in Ephesians 5. I found myself becoming bitter and angry that my husband was more excited about seeing other men on a computer screen than me. This part of my "it" was the most difficult to accept. A woman would have been hard, but the fact that he was more excited to see men hurt to the core. I was not living the abundant life that Jesus promised in John 10:10 (NKJV), saying "The thief does not come except to steal, and to kill, and to destroy. I have come that they may have life, and that they may have *it* more abundantly." I was coping with the thief in my marriage that came to kill, steal, and destroy. Coping is defined as facing and dealing with responsibilities, problems, or difficulties, especially successfully or in a calm or adequate manner. This defined most of my life. I grew up in a home in which I was groomed to cope. My mother coped in her marriage and was a functioning alcoholic that would drink, but never appear drunk or miss a beat at home. She loved us, prepared food, cleaned the house and everything else that a good mother would do, and she coped with a bottle and died from cirrhosis of the liver. I was educated in coping from a professional that stayed in a marriage that was not conducive to her wellbeing, though my dad was a good provider. I appreciated him for that later in life. But in my own marriage, I finally came to the realization that my husband did not love me. Though I handled our situation well on the outside, on the inside I was coping with the Devil who was trying to steal my joy. My worship won wars for me. I benefited from my morning prayers, my private Bible study, my assignment as prayer warrior, and standing in the gap for others. All of it kept me despite the chaos in my life. My heart was with Jesus, and I can say that when I had the fleshly desire to do wrong, and even the opportunity, the vow that I took to God first and then to my husband, resounded in my spirit. I learned a valuable piece of information from those years of marriage, being a Christian, a minister, woman of God, and laborer in the vineyard. We are not exempt and do not possess any supernatural powers that keep us from feeling and experiencing this "it" called life. But the good news is that God has supplied us with His Word as a weapon to destroy whatever the "it" in our lives. Every negative word that was spoken over us is a lie. If you are at a pivotal point in your life, look at that situation and say, "I can and will recover from this with peace. There is proof of it. 2 Timothy 1:7 (NKJV) says, "For God has not given us a spirit of fear, but of power and of love and of a sound mind." It may be scary now, but understand that the spirit of fear is not from God. It is from your adversary, the Devil. Get rid of it; don't cope with it and don't counsel it. Grab hold of the spirit of love, peace, and sound mind that Jesus gave you. For he is the lover of your soul, who promised you a life of abundance and is not slack concerning any of his promises.

I reached a crucial point in my "it" as we approached our ten-year anniversary. I asked myself, can I do this another ten years? Most people would plan a vow renewal and look forward to the next ten years. Instead, I had to face my "it" head on. I did not feel that God could get his full glory out of my life in a marriage that was not meeting his purpose. I felt as though I was losing ground and my attitude was beginning to resemble one of a nasty scorned woman, a person I had worked so hard not to be. I felt guilty and ashamed, and I experienced these emotions while praying, going to church, and serving. I actually allowed myself to feel and respond according to each emotion. The Holy Spirit reminded me of Hebrews

4:15 in The New Living Translation which states, "This High Priest of ours understands our weaknesses, for he faced all of the same testings we do, yet he did not sin." I decided to take the "it" that the Devil meant for my destruction and turn it into something God could use for my good and someone else's. I decided that my "it" was necessary to move to the next level of glory that Jesus had for me.

Once I felt and dealt with my emotions and the reality of the situation, I had to forgive myself. I could not point the finger at anyone that I thought had wronged me. I had to examine myself and repent to God for all my shortcomings, even the mean thoughts that I had. After the process of self-forgiveness was complete, it was easy to forgive the person that I felt deceived me, and to fulfill my marriage vow until my divorce was final with the right motive. I searched the Bible for scriptures about healing and forgiveness to learn what Jesus taught. I sought wise counsel, not the angry, bitter girlfriend committee. My private worship time was crucial to how I started my day. I listened to what the Holy Spirit was telling me through the Word of God. I did not pull away from God in this season of change, adjustment, and healing. I opened my heart and asked God," What would you like me to learn in this?" I learned from that moment that the responsibility that God had entrusted me with was worth more than a title. I had a charge from God, as a youth pastor and minister, to help the young people and families establish a relationships with Jesus, and to lead them to spirit filled lives and teach them how to become productive adults as Christians. There is nothing wrong with leading as you sort out life, but at the point of my pending divorce and all that I was experiencing, I decided to resign from my position and the church. The people needed to be taught about the Blood of Jesus that was shed for the atoning of our sins, not the blood of a leader who was more concerned about holding a title and leading than the fact that she was hurt.

I was led by the Holy Spirit to be healed by the Word. I allowed only the Holy Spirit to guide me into my truths and the reality of my life, my setback, became a set-up for my comeback. My "it" was not the end of me. I am not telling you that there was anything easy about leaving a ministry after 16 plus years, not knowing where I would go. I did know that I was rooted and grounded in the Word of God. The Holy Spirit has never left me alone to fend for myself, though I may not always know where to go and what to do. I needed a haven, a church with people that believe in the same Jesus that I do. The Spirit of God led me to that place through a family that is dear to my heart and who knew that I needed to be healed and restored to run this race.

My desire was to be used as a vessel of healing and restoration. I needed to be whole. I learned through my "it" that I can recover from "it." I know that sounds very simple for the long experience that I described, but it is valuable. I can now reassure you that although the enemy pursues you through your "it," whatever he stole from you—even if he tries to overtake your mind—you will recover and with double. Surround yourself with people that have a like mind and determination to make a full recovery. You will have joy, not just happiness. You will smile again. You will trust again. You will love again. You will forgive yourself and others. You will actually believe the Word that you read and that you use encourage others. Jesus will turn your "it" for his glory. The "it" that once had you hurting and bound will be used as your greatest testimony to let someone else know that Jesus is a God of restoration and will settle your spirit with peace. You will be healed from brokenness.

Your transparency and willingness to be honest and to remove all barriers to reveal the ugly details about your "it," is essential for the restoration that can only come from Christ Jesus, who is revealed to us in his Word. He promised healing so much that we can confess Isaiah 53:5 (NKJV), "But he was wounded for our transgressions, He was bruised for our iniquities; the chastisement of our peace was upon him; and by his stripes we are healed." Jesus already won the victory over my "it" and over your "it," and gave us the power through his blood to be restored better than we were before "it."

The process of real restoration is often painful. The process of taking off all the old hard paint, sanding and chipping away, and exposing the original color of the canvas may not be attractive. But we must be willing to be transparent to God. We must release every emotion to Jesus so that our hearts can be transformed from stone to flesh. Do not let the Devil tell you that you will not bounce back or that it is too late for you. Everything that you have gone through was necessary to bring you to such a time as this—a time of good health and good esteem that will spring forth because you are everything that God said about you all through His Word. You are the "apple of his eye" from The Song of Solomon and "fearfully and wonderfully made" as the Word tells you in Genesis. Restoration is the time to love who God made you to be and to soar in the purpose for which you were created.

Go forth Daughter, and know that as Romans 8:28 (MSG) says, "Meanwhile, the moment we get tired in the waiting, God's Spirit is right alongside helping us along. If we don't know how or what to pray, it doesn't matter. He does our praying in and for us, making prayer out of our wordless sighs, our aching groans. He knows us far better than we know ourselves, knows our pregnant condition, and keeps us present before God. That's why we can be so sure that every detail in our lives of love for God is worked into something good." This was written before your "it," and when you get to the other side of your situation, the same word is in place. You were made to win despite whatever comes your way. Allow God to work restoration in your life. You can recover from "it."

Chapter 7

Making Lemonade

Paula M. Grange

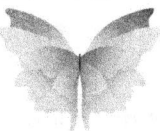

There is an old saying that goes, "When life gives you lemons, make lemonade." Well, I have had lemons of all shapes and sizes throughout my life, and the common fact is that they all were bitter and very hard to face and hard to live with. But God, whom I call "Father," has been true to his promise that he would never leave nor forsake me. The Father has a way of using our life's hardships through a teaching process to bring total healing and wholeness to our spirit, soul and body—for us, in us, and through us—to be a blessing to others. I attended a conference call to learn about this book project, *Born Again Daughters of Zion*. While the meeting was in session, I prayed naturally and I prayed in the Spirit. I continued to listen and prayed in tongues, but I wasn't sensing any direction. I wanted to know if my participation in forming this book was a good idea or a God idea. Some years back, my cousin told with me that she wanted me do something with her, but she was not sure what it was at that time. I did believe that I was one of the women that the Lord had showed her, but when the conference call ended and I still had no confirmation from God. At 7 am on Tuesday, February 6, 2018, I finally began to understand. The Father reminded me that I wanted to speak on behalf of my daughter, Olivia, but no one had ever asked me to do so. Olivia and her dad were killed in a car accident 17 years ago. The accident made headlines in in Baltimore, Maryland because their deaths were among the first reported in Maryland for Y2K. God was going to allow me to share my story via this BADZ book project. I was excited, but I wasn't sure what to say since it happened 18 years ago. I decided to begin with the facts.

Jeremiah 30:17 KJV

For I will restore health unto thee, and I will heal thee of thy wounds, saith the LORD; because they have called thee an outcast, saying, This is Zion, whom no man seeketh after.

Olivia was my only girl and the middle child as of January 1997 when my son, Aaron, was born. She loved her brothers Ron, Jr. and Aaron. Technically, Ron Jr. was my husband's son, but I had known him since he was 9 or 10 years old. His mother agreed and informed me that I was his Mother, too, which was a blessing because he has always called me "Mom." Aaron made it challenging for Olivia and "her" stuff in her room when he started crawling and then walking. She would get so "big sister mad" at him because he would come in and grab anything and try to run away with it. She would yell at him and he would just laugh, calling her "Yvie." She would tell on him and he would tell on her in baby tongues that only God could interpret. I would gently remind her that he was just a baby. And she would tell him that he was a baby and say, "No, No!" I loved seeing them together.

My father-in-law passed away three weeks before the New Year in 1999. His homegoing service was the week before the week of Christmas. My husband had gone to Florida with his brother two weeks before that to help their mom once Hospice was called in. The kids and I took a Greyhound bus to attend Dad's homegoing celebration service because my husband didn't want me to drive alone to Melbourne, Florida with two small children. During the service, Olivia asked questions about death. My father-in-law had been cremated, and she asked me about graves and mausoleums where he was buried, which she called "bed boxes." Olivia was curious, but she was a big comfort for my husband during that time.

I was very tired when we got home from the 15-hour Greyhound bus ride from Florida back to our home in North Carolina, but I had to make sure that Olivia got to her father's house once we were home. I had remarried and her father, Ed, and I shared custody. Christmas was her father's holiday year per the courts. I asked her if she would wait to go after the New Year to spend an extra week with her dad. She told me that she would "let me know." I was somewhat taken aback, but I brushed it off thinking that she wanted to watch the Disney videos with Aaron. I drifted off to sleep and later that evening she came and told me that she wanted to go before the holiday because she didn't want her dad to be alone." I told her that he would not be alone because her grandma would be there with him for Christmas. If I had known what was to come, I would never have let her go. The enemy guilted me most of 2000 about letting her go, until the Word of God began to popped up on the table of my heart.

My husband and I were asked to be in my cousin's New Year's Day wedding and were staying at the hotel with my family and some of the bridal party for wedding. We had all gone to bed. But around 2 a.m., I sensed a very strange feeling that made me sit up in bed screaming, "Something is wrong!" My husband asked me what was it was, but I could not explain because I had never felt that way before. But I knew something was wrong. It was like a breath was taken from me. We eventually went back to sleep, but three hours later, someone came to the door and my husband went to open it. I heard him gasp, so I jumped up and asked what was wrong. The North Carolina State trooper had come to the hotel and told my uncle about the death of Olivia and her father, Ed Thomas (my ex-husband). Early on January 1, 2000, my first born and only daughter and her father were killed by a drunk driver traveling to his home after Watch Night services. She was seven years old. It brings healing to my soul just writing this now, so I thank Father for loving me enough to continue to heal the mother in me. It broke my heart to live life without Olivia Kristen Thomas. "Olivia" means peace, according to the baby book where I got her name. At the time of her birth, I needed peace in my life, and she was my peace.

The state trooper's report said that Ed's car broke down on the side of I-95 and he had called AAA and his family to let them know about the car. They were safe, per the Maryland State Troop who stopped to check on them. He questioned Ed about the little girl asleep in the back seat, but the trooper got another called and decided to leave them because he thought they were far enough off of the highway and AAA was coming to help them. The AAA tow truck driver saw them but he was on the opposite side of the highway. When he approaching the car, he saw that it had crashed into the embankment.

I had no preparation for the tragic death of my first born. I was in such shock that I wanted to make sure that she really was dead. We drove to Maryland on Sunday, January 3rd and three of my close friends came or met us at Olivia's godmother's house. I was told not to be alone when the funeral director came for me to sign the death certificate. I felt the same way I did in that hotel three days before. I screamed and cried when I signed it. My peace, my first born, my baby girl, my pearl was dead.

We flew Olivia's body home to North Carolina. The Funeral director called me to let me know that the non-stop flight had been changed and her body was going to do a layover in Atlanta. This news brought tears of joy because my oldest son, Ron Jr. lived in Atlanta. I called and told him and he was so tickled to know that his little sister came to Atlanta just for him.

We buried her in mausoleum, or bed box as she had called it, days later.

For the rest of 2000 I only wore pink, Olivia's favorite color. She loved Tweety Bird too, so I found and bought 100 angel Tweety Birds and gave them to family and friends in memory of Olivia. I brought jewelry, diamond bracelets, hair, braids, and long nails but none that stopped the pain of losing her. Nothing I bought helped the hurt mother in me. My friends gave me very nice journals and I journaled for a while but it did not work for me because any reminder of Olivia was too painful. It was too early in my grief process to write about it. I even stopped attending my church because I didn't want to deal with the good memories. At the time, I was very active in Bible study and prayer meetings. I was the youth and children's Bible study teacher. Olivia had been right there with me. I could not go back to that church without her.

I appreciated being around my boys during those first two years after her death because I didn't have to deal with the hurt and pain of seeing little girls. I once went to get fish dinners with my aunt and uncle and in came the cutest little girl with her Mom. My aunt tried to distract me so that I wouldn't focus on her, but I looked at her hair bows and barrettes and had to run outside. I waited until I was in the car before crying. Crying was second nature for me since I had a broken heart and the pain of her death was too hard to bear. It was as if someone had stuck seven knives in my heart.

Isaiah 41:10 KJV

10 Fear thou not; for I am with thee: be not dismayed; for I am thy God: I will strengthen thee; yea, I will help thee; yea, I will uphold thee with the right hand of my righteousness.

I went through all stages of the grieving process trying to find peace of mind that seemed so very hard to obtain—hourly and daily. The first year was the hardest because I had no parenting skills that taught me how to live life without my child. I even told God that if did not get any glory out this, I just wanted to wake out of this awful dream and have Olivia back. During the first year after Olivia's death, I would go and call for her to come in from playing. I was just so used to her being there when it was time for dinner. My neighbor would smile and say "It's okay Paula, You can call for Olivia anytime you want."

I planted flowers in front of my house, all pink flowers in memory of Olivia. Digging and pulling the weeds became such a great mind release for me that I would do other people's yards effortlessly and very fast. I did my neighbors' yards, my aunt's, and co-workers'. Gardening was something I had shared with my grandmother. She had a flower garden and she had shown me how to pull weeds and care for flowers. After Olivia, it became my fun and therapy. It brought instant gratification. That must have been what my grandmother felt too.

I asked God for 'hugs without words" because I got tired of people trying to comfort me with their words. I didn't want to hear "She is in a better place," "She's with the Lord," and "You will see her again." I knew that. But as her mother, I just wanted her back. I even told God that I knew that her being with him was best, but that was not for real mothers; we just want our children in our own care. I felt like I had lost my job of as a mother of two without a warning and was never going to get my job back, even after asking the Father daily in prayer to send her back. Shortly after my prayer for hugs, I remember going to the hospital to visit my cousin, and a lady passed me in the hallway but came back and gave me a hug. She said that God told her to give me a hug. I knew it was him because I had asked him. "Hugs without words" always seem to come at the right times. Some of the "Hugs without words" givers would tell me that they didn't know why but they sensed God telling them to hug me. I would just smile and thank them for their obedience to the Lord. I liked, even loved talking about Olivia, but I had to learn when and who to share her with.

In June of 2000, shortly before Olivia's birthday, I joined a support group for parents who had lost their child or children. It was a safe place for me. They taught me that the "greater the love, greater the pain," so I must have truly loved Olivia, because this pain still hurts every day. We talked about our children, which was great most of the time, but even more painful for me in 2000 since my child had died the January prior. I hated to see other parents join the support group as their child died in the next few months of 2000.

Isaiah 61:3 (KJV)

To appoint unto them that mourn in Zion, to give unto them beauty for ashes, the oil of joy for mourning, the garment of praise for the spirit of heaviness; that they might be called trees of righteousness, the planting of the Lord, that he might be glorified.

Palms 107:20 (KJV)

He sent his word, and healed them, and delivered them from their destructions.

In 2001, I went churches where nobody knew me or knew that my daughter was killed by a drunk driver. I started doing this because my husband asked me to go back to church. He knew my life as a firm believer, and he knew that I had been out of church life for too long. I shared this with my friend who also had loss her child a few years before the death of Olivia. She shared how she would just go and sit in the back of her church to be in the presence of the Word of God. She told me to go and just sit to hear the Word. She said that I could leave after the Word if I needed to avoid the people. I really loved attending church like this because I did not have to act strong or pretend that I was alright because no one knew me and no one knew that my daughter was killed by a drunk driver. This was the first time that I felt like the lemons in my life were cut and being squeezed enough to make at least a glass of lemonade with God's sweetness. During one service, a lady came up to me and gave me a hug –yes, a Hug without words. After that, I felt comfortable to share my story with her. I told her before the service started and she reacted as though it hurt her feelings that it happened to me. She had never lost a child and became very emotional, and other ladies came over to us, too. During the service, the man of God was ministering the word from Isaiah 61, about the Garment of Praise. He proceeded through the congregation, putting the garment of praise on people. I prayed that he would not come to me, but he did. But I thank the Father, because I needed that!

In July of 2000, Aaron and I went to a church per an invitation from the young man who had sold me my Olivia tennis bracelet, replacing one that my husband had given to me. I had lost it in January in Atlanta, GA. It was a small congregation and they were in Sunday school when we arrived. The pastor said that she sensed that God wanted us to go into praise, so she instructed us to move the chairs back and asked that everybody give God some praise. I began to praise God, and about an hour later I was getting up off the floor. I felt like a burden had been lifted off of my shoulders. I testified about what happened to me and she prayed for me. The Lord sent me to a church that didn't know about my daughter, but was powerful enough to help me through the healing process of grief and sorrow. I loved the experience, but when I got back home the hurt and pain was still too hard for me. I had a broken heart that only Father could fix. But I didn't know how or when. These lemons were too bitter, but I knew he could and would deliver me. That experience was in July of 2000. I didn't go back until Palm Sunday in 2001. It was then that I joined that ministry. I served and was trained there for 12 years. I learned that forgiveness is not an option, but a command. There are five things that belong to God: tithes, the glory, the praise, vengeance, and battles. I understand now that when it hurts, I should just let it hurt. But I also know not to get stuck in sorrow. I am thankful as I go through now. Receiving his love keeps me even when things hurt my feelings. I have stopped trying to be strong. Instead, I give the Father my weakness and He gives me His Strength. I trust the Father's love for me. I tried and it works every time!

Mark 11: 2-3 (KJV)

And saith unto them, Go your way into the village over against you: and as soon as ye be entered into it, ye shall find a colt tied, whereon never man sat; loose him, and bring him.

And if any man say unto you, Why do ye this? say ye that the Lord hath need of him; and straightway he will send him hither.

In 2001, the Lord told me that I would go forth in laughter that will bring healing to people. I would be a blessing to people. I thought it was the Devil and began to bind it. But God gave me a program layout that was entitled, "Making Lemonade," that I began to use in a two-hour theatrical showcase in 2003. I asked Him when and how I would be able to stand before people when I still couldn't look at little girls without crying. But God began to give me character skits and they were totally awesome. I counted 66 sketches, and I asked Him what

He wanted me to do with them. At this point, I begin to understand how to make lemonade the old fashioned way, like my momma and her momma made it. The Father begin to show me parts of these lemons that would become a bigger picture. The Devil meant them for evil, to kill, steal, and destroy me. But the Father was going to use my lemons for His Glory, because I had agreed with this and spoke it. The Father honored me. He knows what He placed inside me. My lemons had to be rolled on a hard surface to be softened enough to squeeze. They had to be cut into halves to be juiced. The water had to be poured into the pitcher, then the lemon juice and lemon slices. The bitter was necessary. Then cups of sugar were added. God's job was to make it sweet enough to drink. Hallelujah! Thank You, Jesus!

My lemonade was in the form of a Bible of comical and dramatic character sketches. I have received more from Him since 2003. I don't consider myself a comedian because not everything that the Father wants to say is funny. But this is my lemonade. I have traveled from Atlanta, GA to New Paltz, NY, ministering visual biblical truth that enlightens and encourages a Word life, a prayer life, and salvation which is healing, provision, protection, and eternal life for every born again believer. The Father used my passion to restore me from the death of my daughter for His glory only!

Paula M. Grange

Jeremiah 29:11

[11] For I know the thoughts that I think toward you, saith the Lord, thoughts of peace, and not of evil, to give you an expected end.

4 HIS GLORY Christian Theatrics was birthed in 2003 and took stage on May 15, 2005 in my first "Making Lemonade" Theatrical Showcase. It does just what Father said that it would do, plus a whole lot more. I travel, ministering event performances. I love serving pitchers of lemonade made by God. And New Year's Day no longer bounds me. I don't honor or acknowledge her death. I celebrate her birthday. I have also attended Watch Night Services since 2003.

Chapter 8

Damaged Goods

LaVerne M. Perlie

Being confident of this, that he who hath began a good work in you will carry it onto completion until the day of Jesus Christ.
—Philippians 1:6

Sisters, I'm here to tell you that a path was set before me full of potential, prosperity, possibility, abundance, and success. I call it my destined place, otherwise known as my place of prepared destiny. For a long time, I had no clue whatsoever that it was already mine! Due to immaturity and just plain ignorance, I didn't understand the value in knowing that destiny included me. My poor judgment missed a connection or two along the neurological current of my thought, hopes, dreams, and wishes.

You see, I discovered at an early age that I was not as confident as I should be. I wrestled with acceptance, self-confidence, trust, and doubt. I found out that the announcement of my birth was initially neither accepted nor celebrated. The end result was rejection and abandonment. My then pregnant mother was thrust out of society, considered an outcast. She lost her job at a church simply because she was an unwed mother in the1960s. Somehow that stigma gave me the label "damaged goods." Damaged goods are considered imperfect. All it takes is one spot of imperfection to get the label damaged goods before the product is removed from the inventory. Damaged Goods do not meet the inspector's quality rating as acceptable, therefore the product does not get the stamp of approval. Depending on the type and amount of damage, the product loses value. If it seems repairable it can be fixed and resold. On the other hand, it can be discarded altogether, labeled as trash or no good. Whoever gets the discarded good must decide how to make use of it and make it appealing again. Sometimes, the damaged good is passed around until it is either used up or transferred into the hands of someone else. So, I ask the question, why would anyone want to have anything to do with damaged goods?

    At the age of 14, I ended up at a crossroads on the path to my destiny. I was introduced to marijuana, and since I didn't smoke it frequently, I didn't think it would be a problem. Not sure which road to take and not asking for advice, I felt like Alice down the rabbit hole of plunder, darkness, delusion, deception, and ultimately destruction. But by age 16, I was quite comfortable on this road. There was an ordained shift on the route to my destined place. You see, sometimes even the craziest circumstances propel you to your next place for a destined blessing. I was attracted to many things at this critical time of growth and development. Just like Eve in the Garden of Eden, I too was caught off guard by an attraction. The object of my inquisitiveness was known as Shirley or cocaine. Just like the friends on the hit television show *LaVerne and Shirley*, we hung out every day. Shirley took me to places that I didn't need to go and connected me with people I didn't need to be with. In school, at the movies, and in the mall, I kept her close to me. She was my secret. We became so close that whenever I went to purchase drugs, others who knew me would say, "Here comes LaVerne and Shirley."

During this time, I was in the twelfth grade. I had participated in a dramatic reading contest, won second place, and received a full academic scholarship to college. However, I was still getting high every day. It wasn't hard to buy drugs either. My neighborhood was a candy store of various substances to choose from, 24 hours a day. Between the shootouts, robberies, prostitution, dope fiends, drug houses, arguments, fights, and overdoses, I acquainted myself with things I should not have entertained. Poor judgment led me to destructive relationships, rejection, abandonment, addiction, multiple failures, unhealthy relationships, and domestic partner violence. In essence, using drugs was a distraction that sent me down a destructive path and resulted in unnecessary dysfunction in my life. I became damaged goods!

A Kept Woman

This path of wretchedness was a seven-year journey, and each year the road got rougher and tougher. During my second year of this cycle, I was in a challenging relationship, one that my grandmother would have called "graveyard love." I met an older guy who really seemed to have my best interest at heart. The truth of the matter was that he didn't know who he was. We were both in love with our substances—me cocaine and him heroin—so truly we were selfish. There wasn't any way for us to enjoy a committed relationship because we were chemically dependent. I now understand that this was part of the process that I had to go through. Abuse was the tactic used to encapsulate me with fear, adding more damage to my complicated life. Control, jealousy, and intimidation stripped me even more of my worth. So between violence and addiction, I was a hot, stinking, bonafide mess!

At age 19, after being up for several days partying with him, I felt tired and lightheaded. I went to get some cold water to put on my face. I do not remember passing out, but three hours later, I found myself on the cold bathroom floor. It was then I knew I had to pull myself together because I was in too deep. I started to pull away from him and he became paranoid, thinking I was seeing someone else—although he was seeing two other ladies. He was very possessive, and we fought like Ike and Tina Turner.

Our last fight was my final attempt to get away. He hit me hard because I had taken some product from him without asking, and used it. This wasn't the first time but it was the first time I was caught. I felt like I had just done a Lucky Charms cereal commercial because I saw "pink hearts, yellow moons, orange stars, green clovers, blue diamonds, AND purple horseshoes." I remember ducking and he struck me in the back of my head at the base of my neck. I felt dizzy and nauseated, and my vision was blurred. I grabbed a trophy I had in the house and hit him. I missed his face but got his collarbone, and he hollered. I kicked him in his scrotum as hard as I could and he yelled again. After he collected himself, I ran upstairs. He followed me. I was headed for the door when realized I was in my own house. He needed to go, not me! I told him to leave and not to call or page me anymore. I packed my things, got a hack (now called an UBER), and stayed at a friend's house until my bruises healed and my swelling went down. A few weeks later he was arrested for violating his probation and had to do two years in jail. God will make a way of escape! He kept me when I didn't have sense.

By age 21, I had lost my college scholarship and was placed on academic probation. My career plan of becoming a pediatric nurse was getting bleak. My GPA dropped significantly—from 3.7 to 1.2. The college of arts and sciences let me know that perhaps I needed to pursue another career since I didn't take my education seriously. I wasn't allowed to continue with the curriculum. But I still had not learned my lesson. One day I looked in the mirror at my new size (1), 88-pound frame, and my baggy jeans. The biggest thing on me was my head and earrings. In my mind, I was a size 3-5, weighing 115 lbs. and doing well.

The last two years of this downward spiral (ages 22-23) were the best years of this struggle. Yes, I say the best years because reality was as real as it could get. The abusive relationship had ended, but I was sinking deeper into the realm of narcotic dependence and everything associated with it. I remember going to the store to get a couple of loose Newport cigarettes and as I walked by the neighborhood pharmaceutical sales reps (you know who they were), one of the guys yelled out, "Hey, LaVerne I've got something. It will make you feel good." I got my cigarettes and kept on moving. I held my head up high and acted like I didn't hear or see him or anyone else in the vicinity. My reputation was ruined. I honestly do not remember how I got through some of those days, but I went to work. I went, ashamed and struggling. There was no one to blame but myself. I was not forced into this life; I voluntarily seized the wrong opportunity. One day I left work for lunch and returned an hour and 45 minutes later. When I returned, my supervisor met me at the door. She said that I was being docked, but

God covered my job. Even with the table that was set in front of me, with multiple enemies, God showed me that no evil would overtake me. He loved me for real! I am a kept woman! God assured me reconciliation, deliverance, wholeness, abundance, and prosperity. These were included my destiny. Angels were surrounding me daily. I was not aware of their presence, but I'm grateful. A major a storm in my life was about to end, and I was determined to go through it.

The Eye of My Storm

I saw the storm coming on the road ahead of me. I didn't have time to turn around, nor was there a detour in sight. I had to make the decision to keep going. The winds were tough, the visibility was poor, and the thunder roared ever so loud. It tossed me all over the place. Several times I was blown to the ground, but I kept getting up and trying to move forward. I was determined to reach my destination and never go back. On November 23, 1990, I remember saying goodbye to Shirley, ending the storm of my life. I purchased some drugs on this day. I knew deep inside I couldn't go on like that any longer like. I was about to lose my job due to absenteeism and lateness. All of my finances were being spent on this habit, and I was down to 88-90 pounds, and I only weighed 100 lbs. before entering this life at 16. Additionally, my grandmother's health was failing and she needed my help. I needed to get myself together. Shirley had proved to me that she was truly my worst enemy and not the friend that I thought she was.

When I told Shirley that it was time for us to depart from each other, I realized that things had changed. Shirley had changed from white powder to the crystallized rock that snatches the mind, will, and the good. Instead of being my friend, she was public enemy number one— a yoke of bondage unentitled to my destiny. Her road needed to come to a dead stop without any possibility of renewal, regeneration, or reconnection. Before I knew it, the dark clouds began to fade, and light made its debut. I could see and declare that great things come from damaged goods. Right in the middle, I was in the eye of my storm! The raging force was behind me, the storm was passing over, and my destiny was in view. I had spent too much time focusing on the severity of my storm without realizing how to get through it. This was the turning point in my life.

I'm grateful that God doesn't discard damaged goods. I know for a fact that He takes the waste that others repel. He then repairs the damaged goods and gives it a full makeover so that you will not see any evidence that the damage ever existed. God gives his stamp of approval, making the product fit for its intended purpose. He desires the world to see the outcome of his handy work by taking a mess and molding it into a masterpiece. When this takes place, the product that was damaged is then marketable, profitable, prosperous, and useful.

Greatness DOES Come from Damaged Goods

According to the inspector (the enemy of my soul), I was found to be unfit, rejected, defiled, contaminated, blemished, and deemed unsuitable. But just in time, I landed in the hands of the manufacturer (God). He specializes in damage control. Don't believe the lies in your ears when you look into the mirror and see the truth for what it is! God also reminded me that I was not worthless no matter how much wrong I had done. He said he would rescue, restore, repair, and replenish this worn-out shell of a woman entering early adulthood. He promised that I would achieve the intended outcome that was ordained for my life, and that I would accomplish great things for him. The best truth I learned is that whatever God ordains in your life to experience, you will go through it. Your tests and trials are not only for you, but for someone else. Just when I thought my life was over, God reminded me that HE had started a good work in me and I would fulfill the plan He had for my life. Philippians 1:6 was the confirmation I needed, which assured me that my story wasn't over and restoration was in reach. He assured my confidence by affirming that I am an intelligent woman, worth more than I ever knew and I was worthy of a second chance—actually multiple chances. I was truly a Born Again Daughter of Zion!

The failures of my past haunted me for years. I had to defend myself with prayer, positive affirmation, new relationships, and compliance in order for this 360-degree transformation to take place. A better quality of life is what I needed and longed for. My new start began when I was expelled from college. I had hopes of being a pediatric nurse or a midwife. Goodness and mercy really followed me as I met with my advisor. With tears streaming down my face, a runny nose, messy hair, dark circles under my eyes, and a final exam with the grade 52 in big red numbers in my hand, my advisor said, "LaVerne look at me. This is not the end for you." She told me to call another school that was nearby and tell them I wanted to transfer. "Your science credits are five years old and will no longer be accepted after this year," she said, "so you must do it now." I followed her instruction, completed an application, took an entrance exam, and was admitted to a new school.

I needed a change of pace, so I relocated to a new area of town. I worked two jobs on weekends at a hospital for three years, and attended classes in the evenings. There wasn't any free time for partying or getting high. Times were hard and money was low but I was determined. My best friend shared her food stamps with me. I had many utility cut-offs and eviction notices. I shopped at the Goodwill and accepted hand-me-downs from those who were generous enough to share. Often, I ate the extra meals at work that were going to be discarded so I could eat. Once I paid my rent and purchased bus fare, there wasn't much money left. But I was determined not to go backward. My prayer life changed too. In January, 1993, I joined a new church and asked God to save my life and my soul from hell. I began attending Bible study regularly. I realized the intimacy that was missing in my life was due to my distant relationship with God. I began to talk to him openly about my struggles, mistakes, and the desires of my heart. I kept pressing because I understood that a caterpillar doesn't become a beautiful butterfly until after it is encased inside the cocoon. I knew once it was time to be released, I'd be a beautiful butterfly without any evidence that I was once a hairy worm crawling around. I was about to take off and fly.

At 25, I met a young man named Eugene while at work one weekend. He was visiting a family member at a hospital where I was working. We chatted briefly and exchanged information. We dated for a brief period of time and married in 1994. He is, to this very day, the love of my life. He accepted me, completed me, and nourished my soul. He taught me how to receive love and love myself. I knew he was a keeper and he's still here 24 years later. I held on to the scripture, Philippians 1:6. At age 26, I earned my diploma in nursing and graduated with honors. I went back to the college I had previously attended to obtain my bachelor's degree. At age 28, I finished with honors. I was in nonstop recovery mode and there was no turning back. At age 33, I gave back, accepted my ministry calling and was licensed as an Evangelist. I served for eleven years as a youth minister, determined to save young people from the pitfalls I encountered. God is an awesome God, and by age 43, I had completed my master's degree with a 4.0 GPA, while working full-time, serving in ministry, and being married with children. I've spent the last 27 years of my life impacting the lives of women and children, encouraging them to live in the liberty that is available to them every day. I'm guiding and encouraging them to make better choices and informed decisions about their future. I am an author, consultant, and new business owner. I enjoy pouring oil into empty vessels until they're running over. New mercies I have received from God. God is letting the world see His new thing! As Isaiah 43:19 (NIV) says, "See I am doing a new thing! Now it springs up; do you not perceive it? I am making a way in the wilderness and streams in the wasteland." And guess what! I'm not done yet this is only the beginning.

We all have a story to tell. I believe that what you do with your story is a good indicator of how you begin to apply the lessons learned from the situation that you encountered. Are you willing to help another sister out? Remember too, that the very thing you need to cope with the situations in life resides within you. I didn't realize that I was confident and assertive, but I didn't need for anyone to affirm those things in my life. I didn't have to be a prisoner to false hope, unfruitful realities, and negative returns. You've got to learn how to use what is within you to obtain what you desire the most. It's called investing in yourself. How do you accomplish this? Faith, prayer, trust, and listening and obeying God. Expect the impossible while you're going through. Never underestimate the power of God's favor, mercy, and compassion. Open your mouth and tell God all about it. That is what I did on Nov 23, 1990. I look into the mirror now and I say to myself, WOW! I think of the words from a song my grandmother used to sing, *"Look where He's brought me from; He brought me out of the darkness, I'm walking in the light. Look where he's brought me from!"*

Conclusion

Charge for the Born Again Daughter of Zion

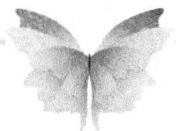

After God healed my wounds and said I was no longer an outcast, I thought about my walk on this road called life. As crazy as it was, all of the twist and turns were part of the plan to get someone else to their abundant place. Abundance is not always associated with monetary entitlements, but it's a peace that makes a woman fertile. Yes, that means you! Fertility gives you the right of way to be impregnated with possibilities, potential, purpose, and promise despite the pain. Fertility gives way for implantation, incubation, development, and growth. It doesn't take a lifetime to catch this either. Abundance is the product of God's favor over your life. Everything that you are destined to become takes place at the appointed time. When it's time for delivery, you'll understand that the pain was necessary, and the rebirth you're about to experience will ultimately reveal who you truly are, who you are called to be, and why you still exist, despite it all. How do I know? You're reading this now! And since you're reading this today, I charge you! I charge you, Born Again Daughter of Zion to:

- Pray daily.
- Move from hurt to healing.
- Walk ostentatiously into your destiny.
- Forgive yourself, those whom you have hurt, and others who hurt you.
- Take your place on top; it's prepared for you.
- Finish what you start and finish strong!
- Love yourself first. It's cool; you're not selfish, just wise.
- Take a look in the mirror and blow yourself a kiss.
- Pursue happiness and positive atmospheres.
- Annihilate destructive thoughts and doubt concerning you.
- Don't stop until you achieve what you're striving for.
- Stay out of the box.
- Own your greatness.
- Celebrate your victories.
- Deny self-deception, and pessimism.
- Be about that prosperous life!

Sources

Unless otherwise indicated, scripture quotations are from the Holy Bible, King James Version. All rights reserved.

Scriptures marked ESV are taken from English Standard Version®. Copyright © 2001 by Crossway, a publishing ministry of Good News Publishers. All rights reserved.

Scriptures marked MSG are taken from The Message®. Copyright © 1993, 1994, 1995, 1996, 2000, 2001, 2002. Used by permission of NavPress Publishing Group.

Scriptures marked NIV are taken from the New International Version®. Copyright © 1973, 1978, 1984, 2011 by Biblica, Inc.™. All rights reserved.

Scriptures marked NKJV are taken from the New King James Version®. Copyright © 1982 by Thomas Nelson. All rights reserved.

About the Authors

Linda Caldwell-Boykin is an entrepreneur in Maryland. She is the proud owner of Salon Spirit, LLC, where she has operated as the Senior Cosmetologist since 2010. She has accomplished great success in transforming lives with creative looks for over 20 years. Her profession has served as a catalyst for a greater purpose, helping those who have been broken and shattered by life's darkest moments. She is known for engaging conversations that inspire individuals to rise from the ashes and embrace their God given greatness. Linda Caldwell-Boykin also holds a Bachelor's of Ministry degree and is currently studying to receive a Master of Ministry degree at Virginia Bible College in Dumfries, Virginia. Linda is the only female recipient of Radio One's 2018 Ministry in the Community award, which honored 20 Pastors for their ministry in the Community. When she isn't helping others to navigate through life, she enjoys spending time with her husband.

To learn more, contact Linda Caldwell-Boykin at Ambassador4ChristMinistryLCB@gmail.com

About the Authors

Carla FB McCray, a native of Charlottesville, Virginia, is a devoted wife, mother of four, and inspirational speaker whose desire is to serve God and his people. Compelled by the progression of her life—from getting married and becoming a widow, to raising 2 children as a single mother, finding love and re-marrying again—she flourished and gained a true passion for working with women and girls through what she calls the three E's: Encouraging, Empowering and Equipping! It has become one of her missions to ensure not only that women and girls understand their true worth holistically, but that they wear their crowns proudly, owning them, embracing them, and loving them. With daily reflection, she understands that through Christ, all things are possible. It is her prayer that God's spirit continues to lead her footsteps on the path to His fulfilling purpose for her life.

To learn more, contact Carla McCray at
Carla.McCray@crownofworth.com

Pastor Jackqueline R. Easley is the Senior Pastor of Faith & Love Christian Ministries, where she serves the people of God along with her husband Pastor Marvin E. Easley. Pastor Jackqueline has a blended family, which includes 4 sons, one daughter, and eight grandchildren. She is a Nurse Educator with emergency medicine experience at Johns Hopkins Hospital, where she been employed for over 25 years. She graduated from Walden University with a Master of Science in Nursing.

In 2006, she faced her biggest struggle, the loss of her son Shelton to violence. As God began to restore her to wholeness, she organized and birthed her first women's ministry, "God's Woman, Equipping Women to Love & Restore," and later founded the Shelton Smyles Foundation, a youth mentoring program for boys and girls ages 8-18, founded in 2014, honor of her son Shelton LeMarr Turner. Pastor Jackqueline's mission is to help others identify their potential in God and help bring wholeness to a lost nation.

To learn more, contact Jackqueline R. Easley at flcmpastor1@gmail.com

About the Authors

Lady Tawanda Holmes is a pastor's wife from Baltimore, Maryland. She has served on various ministries, including women's ministry, and teaches at church conferences and retreats. Tawanda is the founder/president of the Maryland Covenant of Minister's Wives, Inc., a non-profit established in 2014 to mentor ministers' wives and provide community service. She is also a CPA and provides financial advice to local churches. Tawanda served in the U.S. Navy Reserves for 18 years and has been employed with the federal government since 1988. She also taught at the Baltimore City Community College for five years. She has a Bachelor of Science in Accounting, a Master of Arts in Professional Studies, and graduated from the Baltimore School of the Bible. Tawanda and Pastor Eugene B. Holmes, Jr. were married in 2004 and together they have six children and seven grandchildren.

To learn more, contact Tawanda Holmes at
Ladyhbmbc@gmail.com.

Michelle Baylor holds an associate degree in Spanish and a bachelor's degree in Christian Education. She is a veteran of the United States Army, having served active duty for eight years in the field of Intelligence. In her spare time, Michelle serves as a nursing home and hospice volunteer. She enjoys studying the word of God and looks for every opportunity to talk to others about God's grace. She understands that life's experiences can put us in bondage that can imprison the mind, body, and spirit, and as a Christ follower, fitness enthusiast, and a certified personal trainer, Michelle protects her whole being from life's challenges. Michelle is a very content resident of Parkville, Maryland. She enjoys her retirement by traveling, working out in the gym, attending various recreational and cultural events, and spending time with her children, grandchildren, other family members, and friends.

About the Authors

Arvinese I. Reid is a minister at The Tabernacle of Prayer Revival Center in Dobbs Ferry, New York. A dedicated woman of God, she is passionate about her ministry and her mission to be used by God as a vessel to reveal the restorative power of Jesus Christ. She believes in empowering others to know that they can overcome any obstacles and setbacks in life. When Arvinese is not ministering the gospel, she is enjoying her family.

Arvinese obtained an associate degree in liberal arts, a certificate in paralegal studies, and will graduate with a Bachelor of Science in Human Service in 2019. She is a resident of Garnerville, New York, and is the mother of one daughter, Aaliyah Slaughter, and two grandchildren, Tori and Terrance Newland.

Paula M. Grange is an actress and entertainer, and the founder of 4 HIS GLORY Christian Theatrics. Her one-woman performances and theatrical showcases visually minister the Word of God with a little touch of "DRAMA."

Paula attended Winston-Salem State University where she reigned as Miss WSSU in 1984 and earned a Bachelor of Science in Computer Science. It was as a freshman in 1980, on the WSSU campus, that she gave her life to Christ. Paula is an IT professional by trade but is also an evangelist, licensed by the late Apostle Robert Battle of Tabernacles of Worship Christian Church, Bowie, MD. She believes in a Word life and a prayer life.

Her Favorite Scripture: "Trust in the Lord with all thine heart and lean not unto thine own understanding. In all thou ways acknowledge him, and he shall direct thy paths (Proverbs 3:5-6 KJV).

About the Authors

LaVerne M. Perlie is a dynamic and multifaceted wife, mother, nurse, author, and preacher. Her passion is encouraging and inspiring women and children through her testimony to have an improved quality of life, despite experiencing relentless challenges. LaVerne enjoys serving others, watching lives transform, and building partnerships in her community. She is the Founder and Executive Director of Flame of Fire Ministries, a non-profit organization serving women and at-risk youth to help improve their quality of life. Flame of Fire Ministries provides workforce development training for women recovering from addiction, college preparation, scholarship, mentoring, and leadership development for middle/high school aged males. LaVerne is an ordained Elder who develops evangelism plans for urban communities, coordinates discipleship classes, and oversees the strategic plans for several church ministries. Her scripture for living is Romans 8:31 (KJV) "What shall we then say to these things? If God be for us, who can be against us?"

To learn more, contact LaVerne Perlie at
https://badzherstory.com or by email at Pevangel@live.com

CREATING DISTINCTIVE BOOKS WITH INTENTIONAL RESULTS

We're a collaborative group of creative masterminds with a mission to produce high-quality books to position you for monumental success in the marketplace.

Our professional team of writers, editors, designers, and marketing strategists work closely together to ensure that every detail of your book is a clear representation of the message in your writing.

Want to know more?
Write to us at info@publishyourgift.com
or call (888) 949-6228

Discover great books, exclusive offers, and more at
www.PublishYourGift.com

Connect with us on social media

@publishyourgift

www.ingramcontent.com/pod-product-compliance
Lightning Source LLC
Chambersburg PA
CBHW052149110526
44591CB00012B/1908